Marketing Planning for the Pharmaceutical Industry

Second Edition

Publications by the same author:

Beyond the Pay Packet (1992), McGraw-Hill
Face the Press (1992), Nicholas Brealey
How to Recruit and Select Successful Salesmen (2nd Edn) (1983), Gower
Making Effective Presentations (Audio manual) (1985), Gower
Manual of Sales Negotiation (1991), Gower
Marketing Planning for the Pharmaceutical Industry (1987), Gower
Motivating Your Sales Force (1978) (paperback, 1995), Gower
Negotiating Profitable Sales (1977), Gower; also handbook (for Video Arts) of the same title (1979), Video Arts
The Sales Presentation (jointly) (1985), Gower
Training Salesmen on the Job (2nd edn) (1986), Gower; also handbook (for Rank Films) of same title (1981), Rank Aldis

Marketing Planning for the Pharmaceutical Industry

SECOND EDITION

JOHN LIDSTONE

in association with
JANICE MACLENNAN
St Clair Consulting Ltd

Gower

First published 1987 by Gower Publishing Company Limited

Published by
Gower Publishing Limited
Gower House
Croft Road
Aldershot
Hampshire GU11 3HR
England

Gower
Old Post Road
Brookfield
Vermont 05036
USA

John Lidstone has asserted his right under the Copyright, Designs and Patents Act 1988 to be identified as the author of this work.

British Library Cataloguing in Publication Data

Lidstone, John, 1929–
    Marketing planning for the pharmaceutical industry. – 2nd ed.
    1. Health facilities – Marketing
    I. Title II. Marketing planning for the pharmaceutical
    industry
    362.1'0688

ISBN 0 566 08112 1

Library of Congress Cataloging-in-Publication Data

Lidstone, John, 1929–
    Marketing planning for the pharmaceutical industry / John Lidstone, in
    association with Janice MacLennan.
        p.   cm.
    ISBN 0–566–08112–1 (hc.)
    1. Medical care—Marketing—Planning.   I. MacLennan, Janice.
    II. Title.
    RA410.56.L53   1999
    362.1'068'8—dc21   98–41233
                                                                        CIP

Typeset in Caslon by Bournemouth Colour Press, Parkstone and printed in Great Britain by the University Press, Cambridge.

Contents

List of Figures   ix
List of Tables   xi
Foreword   xiii
Preface   xv
Acknowledgements   xix
About the Authors   xxi

1   INTRODUCTION   1
What is meant by the term 'marketing plan'?   1
Why marketing planning?   1
How do marketing plans accommodate the future?   1
The benefits of planning   2
The marketing planning concept   3
The marketing planning process   5
The fit with company objectives, structure and planning stages   8
Why a handbook of pharmaceutical marketing planning?   10
Format of a marketing plan   12
Information required   12

2   THE EXTERNAL ANALYSIS   15
Establishing a customer focus   15
Market segmentation   16
The market analysis   22
Undertaking the environmental analysis   30
How to approach the environmental analysis   33
Interpreting opportunity and threats   34

3   THE INTERNAL ANALYSIS   37
The search for competitive advantage   37
The product audit   38
The company audit   41
Interpreting strengths and weaknesses   47

4 THE SWOT ANALYSIS 49
What is a SWOT analysis? 49
Why do you need a SWOT analysis? 49
How to build a SWOT analysis 50

5 PRODUCT STRATEGY 61
Introduction 61
Definition of terms used 61
Generating the strategic options 63
Selecting a strategy 67

6 SALES FORECASTING AND STRATEGY 71
Introduction 71
Why forecasting is important 72
The market forecast 73
The product forecast 75
Sanity checking the sales forecast 78
The quarterly review 80
Expenditure forecasting 81
Sales forecasting methods – an overview 83

7 STRATEGY IMPLEMENTATION 87
Introduction 87
Critical success factors 87
Setting marketing objectives 89
The tactical plan 90
The role of the product manager 91

8 COMMUNICATIONS AND ITS ROLE IN STRATEGY IMPLEMENTATION 93
The promotional mix 94
Deciding on the creative strategy 94
The communications process 99
Integrating the other elements in the marketing mix with promotion 101
The role of the external agency 103
Communications agencies' perspectives of the pharmaceutical industry 105

9 MARKETING RESEARCH 113
The marketing research process 113
Types of research 114
The use of an external agency 119
The market researchers' perspective of the pharmaceutical industry 120

10 IMPLEMENTATION AND CONTROL 125
Introduction 125
Product profit-and-loss statement (P.&L.) 126
Summary of key objectives/actions 126
Performance feedback 126

11   WRITING THE PLAN   133
   The importance of writing in business   133
   Prepare before you write   133
   Basic formats   134
   Words, sentences, paragraphs, facts and tables   134
   A checklist for effective writing   135
   A template for the marketing plan   136

Glossary of Marketing Terms   137
Index   143

List of Figures

1	The marketing planning process	4
2	A different perspective of the marketing planning process	5
3	Eight-stage marketing planning cycle	9
4	Operation of the planning cycle	11
5	Bases for segmenting markets	18
6	Flow of buying decision	20
7	The potential market	23
8	Growth/share matrix	28
9	The product positioning analysis (an example)	39
10	A perceptual map for OTC analgesics	40
11	The strategic decision grid	55
12	The traditional SWOT	57
13	The Ansoff Matrix	64
14	Porter's Competitive Strategy Model	65
15	Performance/importance matrix	88
16	The decision-making process	97
17	Agency evaluation criteria	106
18	A marketing research decision-making process	115
19	The Z-Chart	131

List of Tables

1	Market potential and opportunity	25
2	Competitor performance – volume analysis (Rx, etc.)	26
3	Competitor performance – value analysis (Av price/Rx, etc.)	27
4	Identify the key trends	35
5	Evaluating their impact at a segment level	36
6	Capabilities that might provide a source of competitive advantage	43
7	Example company audit	46
8	SWOT analysis	53
9	Interpretation of the issues	58
10	Definition of terms used	62
11	Forecasting impact of key trends	75
12	Adjusting market growth according to strategy	76
13	Forecasting the product sales	77
14	Strengths/weaknesses analysis	88
15	Marketing Action Plan template	90
16	Promotional mix options	95
17(a)	Advantages and disadvantages of data collection methods	117
17(b)	Advantages and disadvantages of postal collection methods	117
17(c)	Advantages and disadvantages of telephone collection methods	117
18	Annual sales forecast	127
19	Marketing profit statement	128
20	The Action Plan	129

Foreword

by Franz B. Humer, CEO, F. Hoffmann-La Roche

There are very few business books that fall into the category 'classic'. So many representing fashionable fads are soon forgotten. *Marketing Planning for the Pharmaceutical Industry* is undoubtedly a classic, updated from its 1987 predecessor.

Business fundamentals, such as good segmentation, branding, opportunity analysis and strength definition, do not go out of date. They do, however, often disappear from managers' minds, and it is here that John Lidstone's book plays such an important role.

In one concise volume, specifically related to the Pharmaceutical and Healthcare industries, the author has assembled an A to Z of how to plan and execute product strategy successfully. The outlined systematic, yet simple, approach, will be invaluable both to new and experienced managers.

Of particular value will be the section on market segmentation – a concept that has traditionally been poorly applied in our industry. With the coming of a new technological era driven by pharmacogenomic research and marketing, required skills such as segmentation analysis will find managers reaching for their bookshelves. John Lidstone's 'classic' will be near the top of the list.

Basel 1998

Preface

The world in which pharmaceutical industry marketing executives operate has changed dramatically since my book *Marketing Planning for the Pharmaceutical Industry* was first published in 1987.

In 1965 I made a forecast that, within twenty years, the industry would be dominated by ten major companies. I was a little out in my timing, but not by much. Yet, even as I write these lines, there are rumours of mega mergers among those top ten. To illustrate my point, in the acknowledgements in the first edition, I listed 45 companies whose managements I had advised on marketing strategy between 1965 and 1987. As industry companies have grown larger in size but fewer in number, 23 of those 45 companies have since merged, been taken over, or gone out of business. Flowing from these changes, *five* key developments can be identified, all with serious implications for senior managers.

1. The concentration of companies has led to flatter organizational structures. Managers now have to look after larger teams, leaving them with little or no time for on-the-job training and individual skills development. Learning how to market by 'sitting next to Nellie' has become more commonplace than was true 11 years ago, especially in these massive companies, with all the consequent dangers. The grey heads that were around to help new young marketers in the early years of their careers, have all gone.
2. The shift towards 'business management' has produced more confusion than clarity. Questions being raised include: 'Should strategy be driven from the bottom up? Should marketing be regionalized? If so, when? why? and, how do we do it?'
3. The difference between marketing and communication strategy is poorly understood. A marketing strategy needs to be agreed and in place before the communication strategy can be developed.
4. Branding is still not adopted. Why? Because drugs are not seen as a suitable vehicle for it.
5. In the current cost-constrained environment money can no longer buy success. Understanding your customers and their needs, combined with smart marketing principles, are some of the essential keys for success.

As we approach the millennium, the computerization of so many marketing and sales activities should have released more time for managers to have hands-on management. Paradoxically, the reverse has happened. The high cost of keeping a sales force on the road might, just might, have led to smaller, more tightly focused sales teams. But, no: armies of salespeople now hurl themselves into dialogue with the medical profession.

For all these reasons, healthcare companies whether they work in pharmaceuticals, biotechnology, medical equipment, medical insurance, or hospitals, need to ensure that realistic, challenging plans are developed, then implemented by marketing and sales executives who have been appropriately trained and coached, held together in a customer-facing organization, designed for the markets in which they operate.

The purpose of this book

The products and services for which marketing and product managers are responsible are the means by which a company delivers value satisfactions to its customers. For this reason it is vital that you have clear guidelines to help you prepare realistic, individual, strategic marketing plans for them, and, more important, to help you produce a strategy which can be supported by all functions and a marketing plan which can be implemented. That is the purpose for which this handbook has been compiled.

Who is it for?

This handbook has been designed so that it can be used to construct strategic marketing plans by:

● corporate marketing management at headquarters;
● marketing and, especially, product managers.

Like the first edition, which became a standard source of reference, this one is designed to counter the greatest danger to which a product manager can be exposed in a healthcare company, which is: 'If a product is everybody's business, then it becomes nobody's business.'

The product manager can and must take responsibility for a product from the time it is approved, through all its stages, to the ongoing monitoring of its profit contribution, which is derived from being prescribed or used again and again and again. While the core philosophy from the first edition remains in place, it has undergone a 'shakeout', designed to make it flow much better.

In Chapter 2 there is a new orientation to the external analysis. The concept and technique of SWOT Analysis, pioneered in the first edition, has new material and new ways of looking at analytical SWOT, helped further by additional diagrams. Chapter 6 on Sales Forecasting is new. Chapter 7, Strategy Implementation contains a great deal of new thinking. Distribution and Packaging have been omitted because, as a general rule, product and marketing executives do not have much say or decision-making responsibility over these areas of company management.

Pricing has also been left out of this edition. Not only in the UK but also in most other countries, pricing is such a political issue in healthcare that few managers have much say, let alone control, over it.

CONCLUSION

Pharmaceutical companies set themselves one of the most challenging and difficult of tasks: to achieve honourable commercial objectives from the results of the scientist's search for knowledge to alleviate suffering and cure the ills of mankind. To do this consistently, companies must plan and organize themselves to create and exploit future market growth opportunities. It is to that worthwhile end result that all strategic plans should be directed. The strategic marketing plan provides a coherent framework:

- to identify potential marketing opportunities and threats, so that the company can keep watch and monitor emerging social, economic, technological, political and competitive trends and changes that could be vital to success or failure;
- for management to appraise the company's portfolio of products and competitive offerings and the financial, marketing, production and other resources allocated to them;
- to identify internal strengths and weaknesses of products and personnel;
- within which to test and conceive different strategies for different markets.

The marketing planning system described in this handbook is not a strait-jacket, but is designed to enable you to be flexible and responsive to warning signals from the environment. It is designed to help you produce a dynamic line-management tool, not a fat document, conceived in an ivory tower, to which no one pays any attention. A market plan is incomplete without hard figures, but figures alone do not make a plan.

Finally, for me the acid test of a company that plans its future and then works its plans is whether all the plans at every level are dog-eared, dirty from constant reference and, by the end of the financial year, covered with notes about what human beings did and how they did it, to close the gap between what was planned and what actually happened in the messy reality of commercial life.

John Lidstone

Acknowledgements

The core philosophy and marketing techniques in the first edition stay at the heart of this second one. They were not only tested, but formed the foundation stones for the marketing planning systems developed by major pharmaceutical and healthcare companies in the United Kingdom, America, Europe and the Far East. The feedback from companies showed that, having been tested at the sharp end, they remain effective and practical.

The comments and constructive criticisms I have received during the last ten years from pharmaceutical companies, industry colleagues, and management consultants the world over, too numerous to name individually, have encouraged me to embark on this second edition.

But, especially, I must single out for mention and thanks Janice MacLennan, Managing Director of St Clair Consulting Limited. She not only encouraged me, but backed her own enthusiasm in the most practical way possible; by helping me to revise those sections of the first edition which needed updating.

Janice also applied her formidable intellect to specific chapters on Sales Forecasting and Strategy Implementation. And, through her work with her company's pharmaceutical clients, she has given a new depth to that major planning driver, Analytical SWOT.

We would like to thank and acknowledge the following people with whom St Clair Consulting have worked, for their contributions to the thinking and advancement of the ideas we have developed: Liz Norton and David Roe, Janssen-Cilag; Pietro Crovetto, GlaxoWellcome; Sue Kewney, Rhone Poulenc Rorer; John Larter, SmithKline Beecham International; Maria Dzaleta, SmithKline Beecham UK; John Bolter, Quintiles; Anne Bradley, National Asthma Campaign; Jo Collett, GlaxoWellcome; Jackie Westaway, SmithKline Beecham SPD; and Jeremy Poole, AAH Pharmaceuticals Ltd (Hospital Service).

The new ideas in Chapters 8 and 9 would not have been possible without the advice and help from a number of colleagues. We would like to thank Elaine Macfarlane, Macfarlane Communications Ltd; Mark Boulding, Money Syner Communications; Leila Wallis and Judy Larkin, Inks Partnership; Mike Owen, Context Research Services Ltd; Kim Hughes, Director, The Planning Shop; Andrew Major, Market Research Manager, Janssen-Cilag.

Although mission statements come in for much adverse criticism, when skilfully crafted they are invaluable in concentrating the minds of all on what matters. I am grateful to industry colleagues who shared their thoughts and their companies' mission statements with me: the management of GlaxoWellcome; Mike Gatenby and David Pilley, Zeneca Pharma; Mike Wilson, Pfizer Ltd; and Bill Fullagar, Novartis.

John Lidstone

John Lidstone

An internationally recognized leader in management and marketing consultancy, John Lidstone retired as Deputy Chairman of Marketing Improvements Group Plc in 1993, after spending nearly thirty years helping to build it into one of the foremost firms in marketing consultancy, research and training operating throughout the world, following eleven years with the Shell Group and teaching at Repton School.

He created and built the group's Healthcare division and directed marketing consultancy assignments for 45 multi-national pharmaceutical companies working for them in over 42 countries. This included developing, testing and installing marketing planning systems from which the material in this book is derived. He is also the author of 15 other books.

In 1993 John returned to the academic world to write the distance-learning marketing modules for the MBA programme of the University of Surrey's School of European Management and as Marketing Adviser to the School of Pharmacy, University of Mississippi. He also lectures on modules for the MSc in Pharmaceutical Medicine and the new MSc in Management Consultancy at Surrey.

Janice MacLennan

Managing Director of St Clair Consulting, Janice MacLennan combines a degree in Pharmacy with extensive in-depth marketing experience in Pharmaceuticals, Healthcare and related disciplines.

From Senior Brand Manager at Beecham Pharmaceuticals, she became a Managing Consultant at a major London-based Marketing Consultancy, where she met and worked closely with John Lidstone. Janice then went on to found St Clair Consulting, enabling her to capitalize on her extensive pharmaceutical and healthcare experience working with multi-national companies throughout the world.

Janice has rapidly built an enviable reputation with major blue-chip clients and is widely regarded as being an authority on strategic, marketing and business planning for all aspects of healthcare and is also actively involved in the development of process and people in the marketing arena.

1 _____

Introduction

What is meant by the term 'marketing plan'?

As with so many terms used within the industry, the term 'marketing plan' is often misunderstood. That as a statement may come as a surprise. Let us justify it. When someone is asked to produce a marketing plan, what is so often submitted is a document which contains data, accompanied by narrative which explains to people who cannot read data what it is the data is illustrating. This is accompanied by a SWOT analysis, occasionally a positioning statement and an action plan (often described as 'the strategy').

What we should see is a clear statement of the goals/objectives, the strategy for achieving the objectives, and a plan that demonstrates how the strategy will be implemented; also, at the outset, a summary of the business situation as we see it, highlighting the issues. This provides the context for strategy for the reader. It also serves as a useful reminder to the author of the plan of the issues which are supporting the strategic choice. If the issues change, inevitably the strategy and/or implementation plan will also need to be adjusted.

Why marketing planning?

The responsibilities of everyone concerned with managing one or more products fall into two parts. One is concerned with *today's business* and is met by the daily functional decisions that the manager makes. The other involves *tomorrow's business* and requires planning. In both parts the manager is concerned with decisions of allocation. Any company has two limited resources: *time* and *money*. These need to be allocated to generate the planned profits.

Marketing Planning Can Be A Key Contributor To Effectively And Efficiently Managing The Business

How do marketing plans accommodate the future?

A decision made today about allocating resources is dependent upon an interpretation of a known set of variables covering some or all of *existing and potential future*:

- customers;
- products;
- prices;
- costs;
- production;
- technology;
- distribution;
- competition;
- regulations.

Managers must have an awareness of these variables, even if they do not have complete information. However, today's known variables become tomorrow's unknowns, and the only thing certain about tomorrow is that it will be different from today. Thus, the marketing planning process must also consider the possible shape and nature of these variables in the future. This is generally sufficient to make good decisions about the optimal allocation of resources to generate today's business and make us equally competitive for tomorrow's business.

The benefits of planning

All too often we see 'little' perceived value in planning. Why? The relationships between the analysis (data), the findings (information), the interpretation of these findings (the conclusions about the situation) and their role in generating the strategic options are often poorly understood.

A good marketing plan will:

- *help to identify and develop the new skills and procedures that will be required in the future*: the skills and procedures that managers have developed to deal with today's decisions are rarely adequate for making decisions about tomorrow;
- *prepare the company for change so that it can take a commanding lead over those companies that merely react*: as businesses inevitably change, so marketing planning helps the transition from today to tomorrow to be smooth and predictable. Planning for changed circumstances provides the single opportunity to gain significant advantages over the competition. Regulatory requirements, product innovation, new technology, standardized distribution and other realities all combine to even out companies. Yet, the same factors which account for market changes also provide great opportunities;
- *provide a vehicle for communicating the changes and their effects in an open and non-threatening manner*: a common belief is that people resist change; this is a mistake. Research has shown that people resist change only when they are uncertain of the personal effect. When change is shown to be beneficial, it tends to be supported;
- *evaluate and reduce the available options to achieve the best chance of success and the least*

chance of error: there is little choice when allocating today's resources and, thus, little room for error. However, when looking forward, the choice is large. R & D can be directed anywhere, plant and production lines can manufacture anything, finance can be raised for any purpose. With such a large range of choice the chances of making errors increase. The alternative is to wait until circumstances change and force a decision. The probability then is that the decision taken will not be the best one;

● *provide a method for handling complexity*: more often than not a pharmaceutical company serves several markets. There are several groups of people who use or buy each product. This produces a complex situation. Each group of people is subject to change, both in varying directions and at different rates. Thus, if a company has only six products each with three user/buyer groups, then it is dealing with 18 different, changing markets. One way of dealing with this is 'muddling through', or reacting when forced to, ignoring the complexity and taking the least possible action. It is through evaluating each market, establishing the nature of the changes and deciding on a profit potential, that resources can be allocated. Thus, the strategy can be the same, but the local market objectives and how that strategy should be implemented will probably always be different;

● *identify the role of each department and offers the means to co-ordinate their activities*: as with changing markets, businesses can become complex. A company with national and international markets may have many departments to cater for some activity that meets the needs of these markets. If all these departments are not co-ordinated and heading in the same direction, chaos will follow;

● *ensure that the company is proactive in its approach to acquiring the capabilities it needs*: as a company develops, so each of the departments evolves; this leads to increased demands upon the resources of time and money. If reactive decisions are made, the resulting demands for plant, equipment, R & D, people, finance, even products, exceed the company's ability to supply. As a result, growth becomes disorderly and wasteful, competitive advantage is forfeited, and profits delayed or lost.

In conclusion, marketing planning is a means of ensuring an orderly and profitable transition from today into the future. If, as a manager, you enjoy letting things happen, if things are good enough as they are, or if you like panic decisions, then marketing planning has no value. However, if you want to *understand and control your growth, improve your profits* or *increase the chances of your company's survival*, then marketing planning is not an option, it is mandatory. Planning is not something apart from the rest of the business. To be successful, it must determine activities and be recognized for what it is by the whole company.

The marketing planning concept

AN OVERVIEW

Generally, everyone is familiar with the key questions – see Figure 1 overleaf. However, there is less clarity and consistency about how one goes about answering the questions. For each question, we consider the answers that might prove helpful.

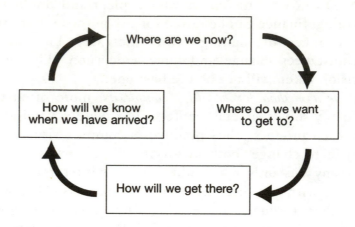

FIGURE 1 THE MARKETING PLANNING PROCESS

WHERE ARE WE NOW?

In a typical marketing plan template this is the section entitled 'The Situation Analysis'. To achieve this analysis, the company must:

- understand who the customers are or could be;
- understand the needs of its customers;
- understand the dynamics of the competitive environment;
- know the strengths and limitations of its own resources, given this environment.

WHERE DO WE WANT TO GET TO?

In a typical marketing plan template this is the section entitled 'Objectives'. To agree these objectives, the company must:

- understand the market potential as it is today and how it is likely to change in the future;
- understand its capability to influence the threats;
- understand how competitive it is for the opportunities;
- have decided the priorities for action (which threats will be managed, which opportunities met);
- allocate resources accordingly.

HOW WILL WE GET THERE?

In a typical marketing plan template, this is covered by the sections entitled 'Strategy'. To arrive at this, the company must:

- have decided the course of action (to whom will the product be sold, how will it be positioned, how will it be differentiated);
- communicate these decisions throughout its management so that the other departments can understand how they can support, and, therefore, what their role is in strategy implementation;
- given the course of action, have understood the marketing priorities for action

(what opportunities there are, what threats, and therefore what is critical to success);

- set marketing objectives against each Critical Success Factor (CSF);
- develop action plans to meet the objectives.

How Will We Know When We've Arrived?

In a typical marketing plan template this is covered by the sections entitled 'Critical Success Factors (CSFs)' and 'Action Plans'. To achieve this, the company must:

- measure actual performance against the marketing objectives;
- measure actual performance against sales and profit objectives;
- revise actions only if necessary;
- ensure there is an understanding by all *why* this revision is necessary.

The key to deriving value from the marketing planning process is creative thinking throughout the process, and understanding the *Links* between the questions – that is, the answers to the first question influence the answers to the second question, which in turn influence the answers to the third question, and so on.

The marketing planning process

The steps involved in planning and their interrelationship are illustrated in Figure 2.

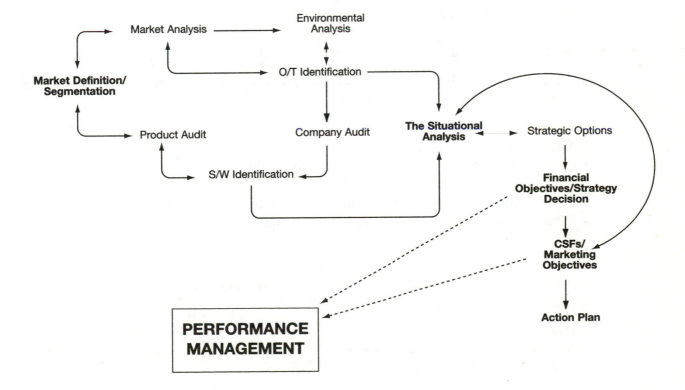

FIGURE 2 A DIFFERENT PERSPECTIVE OF THE MARKETING PLANNING PROCESS

MARKET SEGMENTATION

To derive benefit from this part of the process, the company must:

- identify a way of looking at the market which is different to that of its competitors;
- develop insight in both rational and emotional customer needs.

THE MARKET ANALYSIS

To derive benefit from this part of the process, the company must answer the following questions:

- Which segments are attractive?
- Why are they attractive?
- Who are we competing with?
- How are they competing?
- What might affect the way one should compete?
- Where are the opportunities? Where are the threats?

THE ENVIRONMENTAL ANALYSIS

To derive benefit from this part of the process, the company must answer the following questions:

- What could be the drivers of change?
- What are the likely drivers of change?
- Which segments will they affect?
- How might they affect these segments?
- Where are the opportunities? Where are the threats?

THE PRODUCT AUDIT

To derive benefit from this part of the process, the company must answer the following questions for each segment:

- How satisfied is the segment?
- What is their unmet need?
- How competitive are we with the current product?
- Do we have differential advantage?
- How competitive could we be, through product development/acquisition?
- What are our product strengths? What are the product weaknesses?

THE COMPANY AUDIT

To derive benefit from this part of the process, the company must answer the following questions for each segment:

- How competitive are we?
- Are there capabilities which we have, which provide advantage?
- How sustainable is this advantage?
- How sustainable could this advantage be?

- Through which capabilities could we create sustainable advantage?
- Where are our strengths? Where are our weaknesses?

THE SITUATIONAL ANALYSIS

To derive benefit from this summary, the company must find the answer to the following questions:

- Which are the priority segments, why?
- Where are the priority opportunities?
- Which threats need to be managed?
- What are the issues and why?

THE STRATEGIC OPTIONS

To derive benefit from this part of the process, the company must answer the following questions:

- What are the options?
- What profits/contribution might each option generate?

THE FINANCIAL OBJECTIVES/STRATEGY DECISION

At this point of the planning process, the company must decide and communicate:

- what the revenue objectives will be;
- what the contribution objectives will be;
- which strategy best supports these objectives.

THE CRITICAL SUCCESS FACTORS/MARKETING OBJECTIVES

To realize the full benefit of the earlier analysis, the company must at this point:

- identify what, within marketing's control, will have the greatest impact on success, i.e. achievement of the financial objectives;
- decide how they will measure their effectiveness in addressing these elements.

THE ACTION PLAN

To realize the full benefit from this part of the process, the company must decide:

- how it will manage each CSF, i.e. meet the objectives;
- whether there is an opportunity to do things differently, i.e. are there actions which will provide advantage? Are there actions that could provide sustainable advantage?

PERFORMANCE MANAGEMENT

To realize the full benefit of all the work that has gone before, the company must ensure that they have a process in place that:

- monitors over-/under-performance against the marketing objectives;
- monitors over-/under-performance against the financial objectives;
- requires over- and under-performance to be understood;
- requires action, e.g. doing things differently, adjustment to financial objectives, etc.

The fit with company objectives, structure and planning stages

Marketing activities should be designed to respond to financial objectives, mission statement and overall policies laid down by the board of directors.

CORPORATE FINANCIAL OBJECTIVES

Under this heading should be stated what the company or group's financial goals are which may be expressed as:

- to achieve a return on investment of x per cent over a five-year period;
- to increase earnings per share of x per cent over x years;
- to achieve a return on capital employed of x per cent.

MISSION STATEMENT

This should state what the organization and every subsidiary exists to achieve within the marketplace and environment. It is important to say what markets the company is not in, as well as to emphasize what its specific goal and mission is. This will help to concentrate thought when opportunities to acquire a new company or new products arise. One example of the failure to do this was G.D. Searle. This followed the almost overnight loss of its oral contraceptive business in the wake of the scare that, in common with many of its competitors' brands, its products could be unsafe. G.D. Searle's reaction was to go on a takeover trail, which ended with them owning a variety of companies, manufacturing products as diverse as centrifuges, laboratory equipment and agricultural chemicals. It knew nothing about such businesses and eventually had to dispose of all of them. Then, too late, it returned to concentrate on its core business and was taken over by Monsanto Chemicals.

Here are two examples of mission statements. The first one evolved following Glaxo's takeover of the Wellcome Foundation. When Sir Paul Girolami became Chairman of Glaxo Holdings, he plotted in very precise terms the road ahead into the foreseeable future for the group, based on the following mission:

> Glaxo is an integrated research-based group of companies whose corporate purpose is the discovery, development, manufacture and marketing of safe, effective medicines of the highest quality.

Such a vision not only tightened the focus of what had been, up to that time, a number of loosely-related companies, but led to the disposal of any companies that were engaged in activities that did *not* meet that mission, such as the manufacturing and market of stomabags or baby foods, and Vestric, a national distributor of drugs to chemists and hospitals. Moreover, the money realized from these sales was reinvested in research and development to ensure that the stated mission would be achieved. So far, results testify to the wisdom of those decisions.

In the 1997 Annual Report of GlaxoWellcome, the mission statement of the group reads:

> GlaxoWellcome is a research-based company whose people are committed to fighting disease by bringing innovative medicines and services to patients throughout the world and to the healthcare providers who serve them.

The second mission statement I have selected reads:

> Pfizer is a global research-based healthcare company committed to securing and sustaining the premier position in the world's healthcare market by providing innovative healthcare solutions. Eight core values are critical to achieving this mission: customer focus, respect for people, innovation, teamwork, integrity, community, achievement, leadership.

ORGANIZATION STRUCTURE

Under this heading should be shown the way in which the company or group is organized to achieve the stated financial objectives and mission.

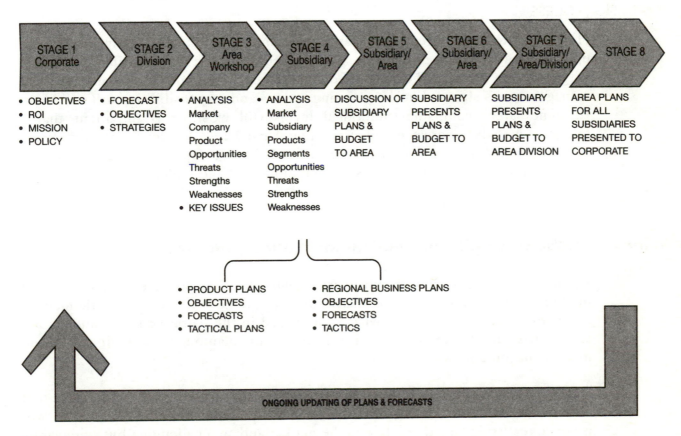

FIGURE 3   EIGHT-STAGE MARKETING PLANNING CYCLE

THE PLANNING STAGES

The planning cycle needs to be as short as possible and understood by all those executives who contribute to planning. The planning process, however should be continuous. An example of a planning cycle is given in Figure 3 (on page 9), which shows the eight stages in the planning cycle.

1. Corporate defines the overall business and financial objectives, confirms/amends the mission statement and the worldwide policies.
2. Divisions/areas make decisions on these overall objectives and strategic priorities.
3. Areas hold workshops when necessary to analyse major market opportunities, key issues and threats, and develop initial market and product priorities for subsidiary companies.
4. Subsidiary companies review initial marketing and regional business plans for products, assess market segment opportunities and threats, develop objectives, sales forecasts and tactical plans.
5. Companies discuss their initial plans with area executives and make amendments in the light of these meetings.
6. Companies present their plans and their budgets to area executives.
7. Companies present their plans and budgets to area and division executives.
8. Area/division plans and budgets are presented to corporate executives/board for final agreement and consolidation into overall company/group plan.

THE ROLE OF LINE AND BUSINESS DEVELOPMENT AND THE PRODUCT MANAGER IN THE PLANNING PROCESS

Having charted the stages of the marketing planning cycle, let us examine how this operates in a typical operational or subsidiary company within a multinational group (Figure 4). In some of the smaller companies there will not be as many levels of management as shown, but the planning actions and responsibilities will still exist. In some larger companies additional levels will exist. It is important that a relationship exists between the plans that have been developed at each level. Furthermore, duplication needs to be avoided. Each company will have a process and it is important that this process is communicated and understood.

Why a handbook of pharmaceutical marketing planning?

In companies with worldwide subsidiaries, managers often produce their own annual marketing plans. In the absence of any guidelines to help you to prepare them, each one is different in size and in what is described in the narrative plans, and, as has already been mentioned earlier in this introduction, planning is occupying more and more management time.

The objective of this handbook is to provide a simple, consistent, uniform system that can be used universally, that will cut down planning time and, above all, will produce realistic plans that relate to the market and are challenging but achievable.

PLANNING	JOB FUNCTION	RESPONSIBILITIES
Purpose and direction of all business activities.	**GENERAL MANAGER**	Overall approval and control of organization. Reports to top management.
Purpose and direction of division (broad strategy and general resource allocation).	**COMMERCIAL DIRECTOR DIVISIONAL MANAGER**	Approval and control of divisional performance.
Marketing and product portfolio information collected, analysed and projected.	**MARKETING MANAGER GROUP PM**	Evaluation and assigning of priorities. Controls planning and implementation of approved plans.
Marketing and product information collected, analysed and projected. Determination of individual product strategies, tactical plans and control of progress.	**PRODUCT MANAGER**	Preparation of individual product plans. Monitoring of implementation. Coordination of product-related resources.
Management and direction to achieve company product sales targets and implement product strategies.	**REGIONAL BUSINESS AND SALES MANAGER**	Preparation of business plans. Monitoring of implementation. Co-ordination of sales resources.
Individual sales activities to achieve sales target.	**SALES REPRESENTATIVES**	Achievement of sales targets and related customer contacts. Provides feedback on local intelligence.

FIGURE 4 OPERATION OF THE PLANNING CYCLE

The great advantage of having a uniform planning system is that time will be saved, because everyone involved will have a common understanding and share the same disciplined approach to the *three* activities involved in developing a successful plan. These are:

1. *Information gathering*: completing the formats concerned with (a) data on past performance, and (b) forecastable trends within a predictable future;
2. *Thinking*: as a result of this data analysis, company marketing executives individually and in groups put their minds to the challenge of finding a way forward. A powerful aid to speed this process is SWOT analysis, a technique to

refine and develop a marketing strategy which will be described for you in Chapter 4;

3. *Writing*: when you do not have any guidelines, there is always the temptation to write too much in a marketing plan. This handbook will help you to firm up quantified objectives, strategies, actions and controls. As a result, the written plan will be much shorter, concentrating on the essential points of the market and product analysis, and thereby facilitating communication of the plan.

Format of a marketing plan

Chapter 11, at the end of this handbook, sets out in detail a model marketing plan format. This will help you in writing marketing plans for individual products by providing a reference to the relevant topics.

Information required

The following headings provide some guidance about the type of information that will be required in order for you to complete your marketing plan. The situational analysis will require interpretation of this information, and it is recommended that it is kept as evidence in the appendices of the plan. Some items, like the market definition, will appear in the body of the plan.

1. *Market definition* – a statement of the market definitions you plan to use: that is, your main criteria for determining your markets – disease, procedures, decision-makers, and so on.
2. *Market segmentation possibilities* – an outline of the way the market could be segmented. This should show the definition and the resulting needs for each segment. Provide an evaluation of each approach.
3. *Historical review* – a two-to-three year historical review of the performance of your market, including major competitors, volume (units, prescriptions, etc.) and value. Tables 2 and 3 are included to help you do this.
4. *Competitive environment* – this should include:
   * a summary of the current key competitive products, highlighting relevant strengths and weaknesses, market share, historical promotion performance, and anticipated future actions;
   * a summary of the new products that you know will appear, including a description, expected impact on the market, and estimated potential share;
   * a summary of the key elements of the company's capabilities and the product features that are or could be relevant within this market.
5. *Socio-political and economic environment* – this will consist of extracts of key facts and assumptions from your company guidelines. The extracts should be those factors that will have an impact upon the market within which your product is competing – that is, inflation, government attitude and plans, reimbursements, public opinion, and so on. It will also consist of any other facts that you are aware

of and assumptions that you are making that do not appear in the company guidelines, but are relevant to the market.

6. *Future Product/Company/Market Developments* – a summary of the major developments that you expect over the forecast period. This will include such things as product innovation, technological innovation, new competition, and population trends, which would affect the market in which you are competing and/or the sales of your product.

2

The External Analysis

Establishing a customer focus

WHAT IS A MARKET?

This is the question that every product manager is convinced that they know the answer to, and one or two of them may even be right! The problem is that most data is available as units bought, units used, prescriptions written, or values. This results in market definitions being confined to the same basis. Yet if one reflects that *marketing is the satisfaction of market needs through your product at a profit*, the fallacy of the typical market definition becomes obvious.

Successful marketing starts with the redefining of the market in terms of the needs of a target audience, and how it is believed they are met through the benefits of products. The founder of Revlon (Charles Revlon) put it well when he said: 'In the factory we make chemicals, but in the store we sell hope. It is the benefits that people buy.'

The market definition is an attempt to describe the full potential for the product by describing who might benefit from the product.

The challenge at the outset is to embrace this market orientation. Given that markets are commonly understood to be those statistics given by audits, the temptation is to adopt a product orientation.

A market orientation ensures that all current and potential future competitors are recognized. It embraces both direct and indirect competition, thereby ensuring that the focus is always on the market need and the possible solutions that exist for satisfying that need. The market definition should also be enduring – that is, it should not change with time unless of course there is a discovery that it offers benefit in a completely new therapeutic area (e.g. Minoxidil, which was initially introduced for men with 'balding heads', but today is also marketed as an anti-hypertensive).

The true scope of the marketing opportunity must be defined before the company undertakes any segmentation exercise. If the full market potential is not defined at the outset the company may find that:

- the definition of the market excludes certain attractive segments, i.e. the full scope of all segments is not known and therefore it becomes clear with hindsight that the wrong segment has been chosen;

- the definition does not facilitate identification of all potential competitors, thus impacting on the chosen segment;
- the company strengths and weaknesses are not matched against the true opportunity – again affecting the choice of the segment;
- the definition does not recognize the interrelationship between the segments, and you cannot therefore consider the development of the market on a long-term basis;
- over a long-term period, management time and resources have been focused on the wrong area (i.e. greater revenue could have been generated in a different segment or, in the case of overwhelming competition, that particular market should not have been developed at all).

EXAMPLES OF A PRODUCT V MARKET ORIENTATION

Brand	Product Orientation	Market Orientation
• COMPAQ	• Personal Computers	• Improving productivity in the workplace • Providing entertainment, etc.
• TNT	• Courier market	• Transfer of information that needs to be protected • The urgent transfer of documents and packages, etc.
• ZANTAC	• H2 Antagonist	• Relief of GI pain • Management of GI disorders, etc.
• PROZAC	• SSRI	• Improves people's outlook • Prevents and relieves depression, etc.

Market segmentation

WHERE WILL WE USE THE RESULTS OF THIS ANALYSIS?

THE WAY IN WHICH WE SEGMENT THE MARKET WILL INFLUENCE (A) THE VALUE OF THE OPPOSITION AND THEREFORE (B) HOW COMPETITIVE WE ARE FOR THE OPPORTUNITY. THE SEGMENTATION APPROACH IS THE BASIS FOR ASSESSING THE PRODUCT-RELATED STRENGTHS AND WEAKNESSES.

What is a segment? The broad definition that a segment comprises 'a group of people whom one can view as having similar needs and buying satisfactions' is a starting point but is not very practical. The task facing the product manager is shown on page 17.

The product manager starts on the left and is continually trying to work his way to the right. This is a constant task of refining and redefining. The 'needed data' comes from market research and will constantly lead you onwards as the segments evolve and

AVAILABLE DATA Market defined in terms of gross units sold		NEEDED DATA Market defined in terms of customer needs and product benefits

change. However, hunting for and identifying needs that your product can satisfy is, in itself, not very practical. In order to take advantage of the segment, it must fulfil the following criteria. A segment must be:

- *measurable:* one can thus be certain of potential and can measure results;
- *accessible:* you must be able to reach it via your promotion resources in a cost-effective way;
- *desirable:* the segment should be large enough to enable you reasonably to expect to meet your objective;
- *homogeneous:* does the 'need' profile of the segment meet the satisfaction qualities of your product?

Segmentation is a vehicle for competitive advantage. Through segmentation you can develop insights into customer needs that your competitors don't have – that is, it enables you to look at the same market in a different way from the competition. Also, in the marketing planning process, all analyses are undertaken for each segment. If you segment the market creatively, you may be able to identify opportunities and threats ahead of your competition.

HOW TO SEGMENT A MARKET

There is a lot of confusion within the industry as to how one should approach market segmentation – that is, whose needs are we actually interested in? When developing a product marketing plan one should always focus on the needs of the end user, *but* as they might be, or are, perceived by the customer (doctor/decision-maker). The role of *customer* segmentation will be addressed later (see Strategy).

Segmentation involves examining groups of potential users to discover whether they have a similar need profile. There are many ways of looking at the groups of potential users. The variables are illustrated in Figure 5 on page 18.

The variables used to segment markets fall into two broad categories: those associated with consumer characteristics; and those associated with consumer responses. There are a number of variables under each.

CONSUMER CHARACTERISTICS

Geographic segmentation: the division of markets into different geographical units, such as continents, countries, counties, cities, towns, villages, etc.

Examples:

- In the US General Foods' Maxwell House coffee is sold nationally but flavoured regionally – the coffee is much stronger in the west than the east.

- In the north of England Marks and Spencer sell different styles and sizes of dresses from the south.

Demographic segmentation: the division of the market into groups on the basis of age, sex, family size, income, occupation, religion, nationality, etc.

This variable is most often used in conjunction with other variables to profile a segment further.

Example:

- Heavy, medium and light users of paint will be further profiled demographically. What is the age, sex, income of the 'heavy' paint user?

Psychographic segmentation: the market is divided into different groups according to social class, lifestyle and/or personality characteristics.

A wide range of markets are segmented on this basis from cars to washing-up liquid, and from furniture to alcoholic drinks.

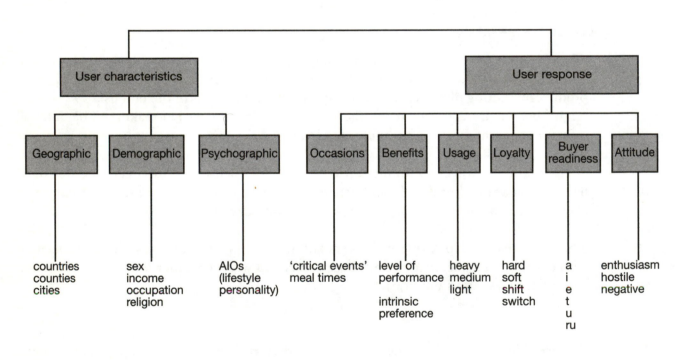

a = awareness
i = interest
e = evaluation
t = trial
u = usage
ru = repeat usage

A = attitude
I = interest
O = occupation

FIGURE 5   BASES FOR SEGMENTING MARKETS

CONSUMER RESPONSE OR BEHAVIOUR SEGMENTATION

Consumers are divided into groups according to their knowledge, attitude, use or response to a product.

Occasion segmentation: consumers are distinguished according to occasions when they develop a need, purchase a product or use a product.

Example:

- Air travel is triggered to occasions related to business, family or holiday.

Benefit segmentation: this is one of the most powerful forms of segmentation, as it classifies consumers according to the different benefits they seek from the product.

Example:

- The watch market
  - 23 per cent of buyers bought for the lowest price
  - 46 per cent bought watches for product quality
  - 31 per cent bought watches for symbols of some important occasion

The 'Timex Watch' strategy was based on the first two segments.

User status: many markets can be segmented into non-users, ex-users, potential users, regular users, etc. of a product.
The difference in the marketing approaches used to communicate with each of these groups can be quite marked.

Usage rate: markets can be divided into heavy, medium and light users of a product. As already mentioned, a product's heavy users generally have common demographics and psychographics which, if known, can be invaluable in developing message and media strategies

Loyalty status: markets can be divided into a number of groups depending on their strength of loyalty.

Examples:

- *Hard core loyals* – consumers who buy one brand all the time.
- *Soft core loyals* – consumers who are loyal to two or three brands.

- *Shifting loyals* – consumers who shift from one brand to another.
- *Switchers* – no loyalty whatsoever.

Buyer readiness stage: markets are divided according to the stage of 'readiness to buy' the product. See Figure 6.

How many people are unaware of the product *v* aware? How many people need to try the product before they will use it? In other words, where are groups of consumers placed on the buyer-decision process, and what should be done to influence each stage?

unaware

aware

interest

evaluation

trial

usage

repeat usage

FIGURE 6   FLOW OF BUYING DECISION

Attitude: people in a market can be classified by their degree of enthusiasm for a product.

Five attitudes can be distinguished, ranging from enthusiastic to positive, indifferent, negative and hostile.

In undeveloped markets, patients have been classified as:

- seekers;
- tolerators;
- avoiders.

Although the previously mentioned segmentation techniques have been used in the consumer markets, the pharmaceutical industry is also finding value in adapting these techniques.

Just from the approaches outlined above you can see the scope for segmentation. However, always keep in mind that the size of the segment is important and do not break down the market to the ultimate degree. The extent to which a market is/should be segmented is influenced by its size and the number of competitors. Even in the biggest markets one would question the value of working with more than, say, seven segments.

WHY SEGMENT?

'Segmentation' is at the heart of marketing because:

- it takes into consideration the customers' needs (the smallest segment is each customer taken individually);
- it provides marketers with a solid foundation on which to plan their resources;
- it facilitates the development of a competitive positioning based on an understanding of the customer's perception of competitive advantage;
- it helps the identification of opportunities and threats (through improved under-standing of customer needs in the target group);
- it provides a precise focus for promotional activities.

SEGMENTATION MYTHS AND REALITIES

The following 'myths and realities' may help to put the subject of segmentation into context.

1. *Myth:*   *Segments are real.* People frequently think of segments as discrete entities whose boundaries are unambiguously drawn, much like geographical units.

   Reality: *Segments are inferred or invented, not 'discovered'.* Multivariate segments are intellectual constructions designed to help explain and predict behaviour. Segments are not, therefore, discrete entities but approximate locations in 'psychological' space. In fact, segment definitions are not totally objective or statistically reliable, and most people embody elements of more than one segment.

2. *Myth:*   *Segmentation delivers only niche strategies.* A frequent assumption made about segmentation studies is that they are intended to identify narrow segments and that users are bound by the methodology to select one target to the exclusion of all others.

   Reality: *Segmentation can actually facilitate the targeting of multiple segments.* Segmentation is often a useful starting point in the development of effective umbrella strategies for a number of different segments. Multiple segment targeting assumes that several segments can be addressed successfully by multiple messages as long as the messages are not contradictory or inconsistent. Each segment generally hears what is relevant to its needs, and may selectively 'tune out' less salient messages.

3. *Myth:*   *A good segmentation study produces startling new or original thought.* Users of segmentation studies sometimes expect them to produce surprising insights and are sometimes disappointed when an obvious or historic segment turns out to be the best. This is often because research cost, complexity and company attention tend to create unrealistic expectations.

   Reality: *Segmentation studies are better at helping prioritize options than at creating or inventing them.* The key virtue of segmentation studies is their ability to validate and quantify the appeals of alternative segments, not to invent them from a zero base.

4. *Myth:*   *Product purchase by non-target segments demonstrates the failure of the segmentation concept.* Critics of segmentation often argue that only targeted segments should respond to positionings derived from a segmentation strategy.

   Reality: *It's unrealistic to expect a perfect correspondence between positioning strategies and marketing behaviour.* Remember that segments do not represent pure typologies: every individual is of more than one mind on many issues. Segmentation should demonstrate a *useful* relationship between attitudes and behaviour – not a perfect one.

5. *Myth:*   *Segmentation is the end point or culmination of a research process.* People who embark on segmentation studies may mistakenly believe that a segmentation study will address all of the information needs – the study may raise more questions than it answers.

   Reality: *Segmentation opens up new opportunities to track the results of a marketing strategy.* Once a segmentation strategy is agreed, further research will be required to fine tune the strategy and monitor its course.

The market analysis

WHERE WILL WE USE THE INFORMATION GENERATED BY UNDERTAKING THIS ANALYSIS? THIS IS ONE OF THE ANALYSES THAT DEVELOPS OUR UNDERSTANDING OF THE OPPORTUNITIES AND THREATS. THUS, THIS INFORMATION IS USED TO HELP US CONSIDER THE STRATEGIC OPTIONS. ANOTHER OUTPUT OF THIS ANALYSIS IS INFORMATION ON THE PRICING AND PROMOTION DYNAMICS THAT EXIST WITHIN THE MARKETPLACE. THIS INFORMATION MIGHT BE USED AT A LATER STAGE TO SUPPORT PRICING AND PROMOTIONAL SPEND DECISIONS. THIS ANALYSIS ALSO HELPS US IDENTIFY WHICH COMPETITORS WE SHOULD BE CONCERNED WITH AND IN WHICH SEGMENTS.

The purpose of the market analysis is to establish the attractiveness of the market in terms of its potential and the opportunities that exist.

It is important to recognize that markets and/or segments which have a large potential may not present a great deal of opportunity, and vice versa.

HOW SHOULD THE MARKET POTENTIAL BE CONSIDERED?

The potential market can be broken down in the following way:

A market is the 'set of all actual and potential buyers of a product'.

The size of a market depends on the number of buyers who might exist for a particular market offer.

The main characteristics which help define the pharmaceutical market are:

1. interest;
2. access.

Applying these characteristics to Figure 7 the different levels of market definition can be described as follows:

- The '*potential market*' is the set of buyers who profess a sufficient level of interest in a defined market offer, but buyer interest is not enough to define a market.
- The '*available market*' is the set of buyers who have interest and access to a particular offer.

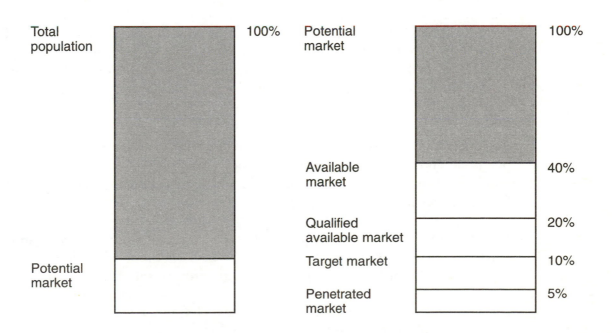

FIGURE 7   THE POTENTIAL MARKET

- For some market offers, the company or government may restrict sales to certain groups, e.g. cigarettes and liquor are age-restricted. The remaining buyers constitute the '*qualified available market*'.

The company now has the choice of going after the whole qualified market or concentrating on certain segments.

- The '*target market*' is the part of the qualified available market the company decides to pursue.
- The '*penetrated market*' is the set of buyers who have already bought the product.

In examining the market potential, one is interested in the total population that could be treated by the product, where they go for treatment, how many end up being treated and what with.

HOW DO WE IDENTIFY OPPORTUNITY?

An opportunity is a 'crack' in the market potential – that is, an area of unmet need. A large market might, at first glance, look attractive because of its potential. The reality could be very different. If the market is satisfied, there is little in the way of opportunity.

A threat refers to anything that is likely to reduce the potential and/or close a window of opportunity.

UNDERTAKING THE ANALYSIS

1. *Identifying the market potential and market opportunity*. In the first instance there is a requirement to decide on and understand the potential. What needs to be considered may differ according to the market. Once the parameters have been defined, and expressed as what you want, i.e. what would make the segment attractive, then *that information* needs to be collected for each segment. A range of data will probably need to be analysed in order to determine the information. The important point here is that the data you need is a function of what information is required, *not* the other way around.

   Table 1 is included as a framework to help you with the analysis. It considers market potential and market opportunity. Typical examples of the information that is required to understand market potential and the market opportunity are included. However, this list is not exhaustive.

   It is difficult to interpret this picture because you will find conflicting information appearing in the different segments. That is, a segment will appear attractive in relation to some of the parameters, and unattractive in relation to others.

   In Chapter 4, we will introduce an analytical technique that will help you process this conflicting information.

   On completion of this analysis you will be able to answer the following questions:

- Which segments are attractive today?
- How attractive are they?
- Why are they attractive?
- Where are the current opportunities?
- Where are the current threats?

2. *Understanding The Competitive Environment.* There is also a requirement to be able to answer the following questions, for each segment:

- Who are the competitors (as defined by the definition of the market)?
- What segments are they operating in?
- How important are those segments to the manufacturers?
- How well are they doing?
- What are their observable brand strategies? And future strategies?

TABLE 1   MARKET POTENTIAL AND OPPORTUNITY

Indicators of Market Potential	Segment 1	Segment 2	Segment 3, etc.
Size of the potential market			
Size of the available market			
Size of the served market			
Av. Rx value			
Trend in value			
Trend in volume			
Indicators of Opportunity			
Market growth			
Number of competitors			
Level of prescriber satisfaction			
Level of patient satisfaction			
Price sensitivity			
Promotional responsiveness			
Level of habit			
Number of customers			
Market complexity, etc.			

Tables 2 and 3 are included to help you identify who you are competing with. The key competitors are those who either hold large market shares or whose incremental market share is significant.

Figure 8 introduces the growth/share matrix as a mechanism for considering how the key players might be competing or what their brand strategies might be. An explanation of how you might interpret the growth/share matrix appears immediately below the growth/share matrix diagram.

Finally, the behaviour of the competitors is likely also to be influenced by the segment's structural attractiveness. Michael Porter has identified *five* forces that determine the competitive environment and therefore attractiveness of any segment(s). The company must assess the impact on long-term revenue/profitability of these five factors.

(a) *Threat of intense segment rivalry:* A segment is unattractive if it already contains strong or aggressive competitors. In addition, watch out for: high fixed costs; high exit barriers; competitors who have high stakes in staying in the segment. These conditions will lead to advertising battles, intense detailing, and price wars.

(b) *Threats of new entrants:* A segment is unattractive if it will attract new competitors

TABLE 2   COMPETITOR PERFORMANCE – VOLUME ANALYSIS[1] (RX, ETC.)

Segment Definition							
	Yr –2	Yr –1	Current Yr	Trend	Growth	Mkt share	▲ Mkt share
Your product(s):							
Competitor products:							

1 Specify the units you are using
▲ Change in market share

TABLE 3   COMPETITOR PERFORMANCE – VALUE ANALYSIS[1] (AV PRICE/RX, ETC.)

Segment Definition	Yr –2	Yr –1	Current Yr	Trend	Growth	Mkt share	▲ Mkt share
Your product(s):							
Competitor products:							

1 Specify the units you are using
▲ Change in market share

who have substantial resources and who drive for market-share growth (*v* short-term profitability). However, if the barriers to entry can be raised or if existing competition will react against entry, new competition may be deflected.

(c) *Threat of substitute products:* A segment is unattractive if actual or potential substitute products exist. Substitutes place a limit on prices and therefore the revenue earned in a segment. This is particularly important in the pharmaceutical industry.

(d) *Threat of growing bargaining power of buyers:* A segment is unattractive if the 'buyers' possess strong or increasing bargaining power. Buyers will try to force prices down, demand more quality or services and set competitors against one another. This threat is a reality in the fast moving consumer goods market where the top five multiple retailers account for between 40 and 70 per cent of product revenue. Companies in this industry focus their efforts on developing superior product offers that the buyers cannot refuse, or enter into a partnership approach with the buyer, i.e. building the business for mutual gain.

The 'buyers' in the pharmaceutical industry are now empowered with their control over budgets, forcing 'suppliers' to rethink their product offering and concentrate instead on offsetting price with brand benefits and market development activities (such as asthma clinics).

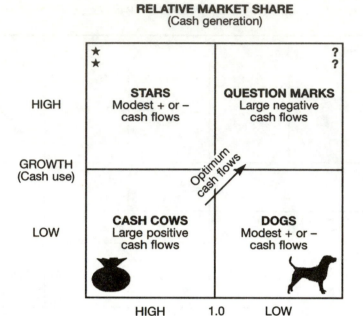

RELATIVE MARKET SHARE
(Cash generation)

FIGURE 8   GROWTH/SHARE MATRIX

Products are entered into the grid according to their co-ordinates of market growth and relative value market share, with their volume represented by the size of the circle. The grid dimensions should be those that most accurately represent the market environment in which you operate. Each of the quadrants has different implications, and a study of the position, relative to the needs and aspirations of the company, will help you to anticipate the company's product priorities.

'Stars' represent high-share products in high-growth markets. These represent the basis of tomorrow's business. It is probable that they will not generate the cash to finance their growth. It is, however, important to maintain support in order to maximize tomorrow's cash flow.

'Question marks' have small shares in high-growth markets and present a difficult problem. They generally generate insufficient cash flow to support growth or even maintain share. So the risk is whether the cost of supporting them will one day be repaid. It really depends upon the relations between high growth and high investment.

'Cash cows' are products with high shares in slow-growth markets. The cost of gaining share is generally very high. Thus, the ideal approach is to provide sufficient support to hold share and use the extra cash generated for other products, such as the 'Stars'.

'Dogs' have low shares in low-growth markets. As a result they generate little or no profit. Any money invested in these products generally does not produce a satisfactory ROI. They also tend to occupy more management time than they warrant. These products need little or no attention and should free resources for use on other products.

(e) *Threat of growing bargaining power of suppliers:* A segment is unattractive if the company's suppliers of raw material, equipment, etc. are able to raise prices or reduce the quality or quantity of offered goods and services. The best defence is to have multiple supply sources and to build good relations.

3. Market Dynamics

The market dynamics are necessary to understand as they will influence the way in which we approach the segment(s). All too often, the industry is guilty of launching a new product into a market without spending sufficient time understanding the dynamics. This, in turn, means that inappropriate tactical decisions are taken.

There are *three* aspects of market dynamics that are of particular interest:

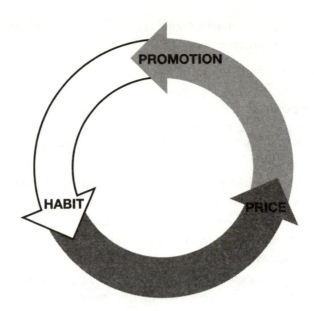

- *Promotion:* The purpose of this analysis is twofold:
  - To determine the level of spend in the market.
  - To determine whether or not the market is promotion-sensitive.[1]
- *Price:* you need to understand where to position your price to be competitive. Some markets are referred to as 'price-sensitive'. Price sensitivity in this context suggests that pricing bands exist in the market – for example, those associated with generic products and those associated with brands. In a price-sensitive market pricing between these bands is dangerous. The territory is often referred to as 'no-man's-land', as pricing here is associated with failure.
- *Habit:* 'level of habit' is interchangeable with satisfaction – i.e. where customers have found brands and/or products that satisfy their needs, this product dominates the marketplace in terms of share. The cost of penetrating a market with a lot of 'habit' is high, and often requires large expenditures over a sustained period of time.

GUIDELINES FOR MARKET ANALYSIS

To conduct a market analysis, examination and analysis of the data must take place so that key findings can be made and conclusions drawn. This means that the data is turned into information. A common mistake is to think that the information is being analysed, when in fact it is only being looked at. The reason for this can be either:

- there is too much data and the manager does not know where to start (because they do not know what they want to know);
- the fact that another department (i.e. market research) has summarized various data into a booklet giving the appearance that market analysis has been carried out (it hasn't).

---

1 Promotion-sensitivity suggests that there is a level of spend below which you get no return for your investment, and a level above which the incremental sales increase does not justify the additional expenditure.

A comprehensive market analysis requires a mix of data sources, together with the interpretation/judgment of the individual.

- Do not be afraid to challenge the way in which research data is captured or reported (especially if you are paying for it!).
- Before beginning a market analysis, try to define the area of issue or interest – this will give focus to the analysis.
- If graphs/tables are used to illustrate a point(s), always explain them fully – for two reasons:
    - Readers should not be expected to construct their own findings/conclusions (they might be the wrong ones!).
    - As time passes you might not remember what point is being made (i.e. explain fully so that the document is an accurate historic reference).
- Remember, do not always judge the commercial attractiveness of an opportunity on value. You may want to consider an opportunity for strategic reasons (to block a competitor, to be able to justify your mission statement to customers and to shareholders).
- If is often difficult to envisage what to include in an analysis for your own brand or in fact a pharmaceutical brand. If you want to broaden the scope of your analysis, try to think outside the industry, and to brainstorm all areas of investigation. Example: If you were asked to conduct a market analysis for BMW, Apple Macintosh Computers or Kit Kat, what would you want to find out and what sources would you access?

Undertaking the environmental analysis

WHERE WILL WE USE THE INFORMATION GENERATED BY UNDERTAKING THIS ANALYSIS? IN UNDERTAKING THIS ANALYSIS WE WILL DEVELOP OUR UNDERSTANDING OF EMERGING OPPORTUNITIES AND THREATS, AND HOW THIS AFFECTS THE FUTURE SHAPE AND VALUE OF THE MARKETPLACE. THUS, THE INFORMATION WILL INFLUENCE CONSIDERATION OF THE STRATEGIC OPTIONS AND ALSO HELP US LATER WITH MODELLING THE MARKET (I.E. MARKET VOLUME AND VALUE FORECASTS). IT MIGHT ALSO INFLUENCE DECISIONS ABOUT EXPENDITURE: FOR EXAMPLE, IF WE ANTICIPATE EVIDENCE-BASED DATA WILL BE REQUIRED, THIS IS AN EXPENDITURE WHICH MIGHT NOT HAVE BEEN PREVIOUSLY BUDGETED FOR, BUT THAT SHOULD NOW BE INCLUDED.

So far, we have only looked at the market as it exists today. However, marketing planning is concerned with change, and change in the form of opportunities and threats comes from outside the company.

The purpose of an environmental analysis, therefore, is to undertake a systematic appraisal of the external environment, thereby anticipating and planning for changes which in one's opinion will have a significant impact on the market. It is probably also useful to plan for changes which might not happen, but if they did, would have a significant impact.

EXTERNAL ENVIRONMENT

There are *six* major components of the external environment.

ECONOMIC ENVIRONMENT

This is critical to the progress of all companies. Its buoyancy affects the growth of markets, as well as one's ability to raise money to finance new or existing projects. Although it is not possible to alter the economic environment, it *is* possible to make reasonable decisions as to its progress.

Key Questions are:

- What changes to the way the government plans to fund healthcare are likely to alter the demand for your product?
- How will the proportion of the total budget spent on healthcare affect the market?

TECHNOLOGICAL ENVIRONMENT

Two aspects of technological advance are of prime concern. First, are there any radically new products likely to be introduced? Second, are there any different distribution or production methods likely to be used which will reduce your competitor's costs?

Key Questions are:

- Are there new technologies that could be introduced that could affect the demand for your product?
- Are there new technologies that might be introduced that could affect the value of the market?
- How will new technologies affect the competitive environment?

SOCIAL ENVIRONMENT

Although the most difficult to detect, changes in the social environment provide the greatest opportunities or the greatest threats. There are two key aspects to social change. The first is changes in composition, attitudes and lifestyle of the population. The trend towards an older population is an example, with its potential impact upon paediatric and geriatric treatments. The second lies in the attitudes and expectations of employees. How will the demands for a shorter working week, equality of opportunity, increased wages or more leisure time affect your company's cost pattern?

Key Questions are:

- What changes in the composition of the population by age are likely significantly to alter the demand for your products (or your customers' products) within the next three to five years? Why might these changes occur?
- What changes in the health expectations of patients are likely to alter the demand for your products within the next three to five years? Why might these changes occur?
- What changes in the attitudes of the medical profession are you aware of that might alter the demand for your products within the next three to five years? Why might this shift in attitude occur?
- What changes in age, lifestyles or attitudes are you aware of that might affect the quality or the availability of your labour force, production workers, office workers or both? Specify.

POLITICAL ENVIRONMENT

In the healthcare market, where the government tends to be the principal customer, the political environment is crucial. Increasingly, government regulation is covering promotion expenditure, licensing, promotion methods, profitability, and so on. These and other factors will seriously hinder your search for profit growth, and must be considered.

Key Questions are:

- Will there be more, or less, government regulation of your production/registration processes in the next five years? What form is it most likely to take? How will it affect your costs? How will it affect your competitors' costs?
- Will there be more, or less, government regulation of your marketing practices in the next five years? What form is it likely to take? What changes will you make as a response? How will it affect your competitors?
- Which, if any, elements of your direct profitability – income tax rate, depreciation schedule, and so on – do you expect the government to change within the next few years? How will it affect your profits? What will you do about it?
- In what ways are you exposed to attacks by consumer groups? (Consider your packaging, pricing, distribution, advertising, and so on, as well as your products themselves.) How serious would such a problem be if it arose? What can you do about it in advance? How about your competitors? What are they likely to do?

COMPETITIVE ENVIRONMENT

The intensity of competition in an industry is rooted in its underlying economic structure and goes well beyond the behaviour of current competitors. It depends on *five* basic competitive forces:

- Potential new entrants.
- Threat of substitution.
- Bargaining power of buyers.
- Bargaining power of suppliers.
- Rivalry among current competitors.

The collective strength of these forces determines the ultimate profit potential of any one market. Changes to these forces need to be anticipated and the underlying cause (trends) understood in order for you to be able to assess how competitive the environment might be in the future.

Key Questions are:

- What is the potential for substitute products to enter this market?
- How might the existing players compete? Are they likely to introduce new products? Or new delivery systems?
- How might changes in the provision of healthcare affect the market and/or your position?

ECOLOGICAL ENVIRONMENT

This may be a surprising area, and yet it is one that has had an effect upon the healthcare market. Greater awareness of products and side effects, concern about constituents (e.g. CFCs), even the resistance to plastic disposable containers, have had recent adverse effects.

Key Questions are:

- What processes or procedures do you use in production that could be criticized as harmful to the environment?
- What would you do if you were forced to change such procedures?
- What processes or procedures do your suppliers use that might be challenged as harmful to the environment?
- What would be the effect on prices and/or availability of raw materials if your suppliers were forced to stop such practices?
- How is your packaging handled after it is removed by the customer? Does this create an environment problem?
- Are there any health-related problems that might conceivably occur among your production workers as a result of the way you produce your products? What are they? What can you do about them?
- Are there any other threats to your operation from the ecological environment? What are they?

How to approach the environmental analysis

In undertaking this systematic appraisal, the following elements need to be considered:

- What is the timescale over which you are being asked to plan? The changes that you are considering must occur within this timescale.
- Have you identified all possible trends?
- Have you used the six headings that appear earlier to check that you have exhausted all possible trends?
- Have you reduced the size of the list on the basis of probability and impact? Refer to Table 4 for the template to help you do this.
- Have you evaluated their impact at a segment level? (Refer to Table 5.)
- Have you interpreted how they would impact on segment profitability? (Volume, value, cost, see Table 5.)
- Have you forecast the scale of impact (very positive . . . very negative)? (Refer to Table 5.)
- Have you considered how this information affects your earlier conclusions about segment attractiveness?

Note, it is not useful to include changes that already form part of the underlying trend. For example: increasing elderly population as this information and its effect on segment attractiveness is already accounted for in the market analysis.

If the environment you are working in is highly uncertain, i.e. you have difficulty in assigning a probability to the likelihood of most of the trends occurring, then this approach is not very useful. Our recommendation in that instance is to use scenario planning as the methodology. Scenario planning is not addressed in this book, but see the reference to it in the Glossary of Marketing Terms on p 141.

Tables 4 and 5 provide a way of collecting and analysing the information.

Interpreting opportunity and threats

WHERE WILL WE USE THE INFORMATION GENERATED BY DRAWING THESE CONCLUSIONS? IN TWO PLACES. OUR UNDERSTANDING OF THE OPPORTUNITIES AND THREATS WILL BE USED TO HELP US IDENTIFY THE CAPABILITIES THAT THE COMPANY NEEDS TO COMPETE FOR THE OPPORTUNITIES AND MANAGE THE THREATS. FURTHERMORE, OUR UNDERSTANDING OF THE OPPORTUNITIES AND THREATS PROVIDES US WITH STRATEGIC CHOICE.

What is an opportunity? What is a threat? The overriding principle is that an opportunity exists for every player in the market, and a threat has the potential to damage every player's business. The options to be considered should not be limited to those opportunities that one is in a strong position to take advantage of. This approach is self-limiting inasmuch as it does not encourage you to consider the full strategic choice.

Opportunities and threats might already exist in the marketplace (this conclusion would have been drawn from the market analysis), or might be ones that you expect to emerge within the planning time-frame (these conclusions would have been drawn from the environmental analysis). Opportunities and threats might be segment-specific.

How should you interpret opportunities and threats from the market analysis? An opportunity is a feature of the market that you desire, and it exists, whereas a threat is a feature of the market that you desire which either does not exist, or the extent to which it exists limits the attractiveness of the segment.

How should you interpret opportunities and threats from the environmental analysis? An opportunity is identified where the key trend is likely to have a *positive impact on the segment*. This could, for example, mean that it will increase the number of prescriptions, increase the average value of prescriptions and/or reduce the cost of competing for the prescription. A threat is identified where the key trend is likely to have a *negative impact on the segment* (that is, the reverse of the above)

Be careful to analyse the impact on *the market* rather than how you think it will affect your product.

TABLE 4 IDENTIFY THE KEY TRENDS

Brainstorm list of trends	Probability of occurrence within planning horizon[1]	Scale of impact[2]	Key trends[3]
●			
●			
●			
●			
●			
●			
●			
●			
●			
●			
●			

1 Evaluate as high, medium or low.
2 Evaluate as high, medium or low.
3 Highlight key trends using a check.

TABLE 5   EVALUATING THEIR IMPACT AT A SEGMENT LEVEL

Key trend	Type of impact (val, vol, cost)	Segment 1	Segment 2	Segment 3
•				
•				
•				
•				
•				
•				
•				
•				
•				
•				
•				
•				

3

The Internal Analysis

Having gathered an understanding of what is happening to the market segments, the next step involves a realistic evaluation of your ability to compete in those segments. Only then do you have all the information necessary to make any definite choice across the segments.

The two analyses which help us evaluate our competitive position are the *product audit* and the *company audit*. The product audit assesses the product in relation to its ability to meet the needs in each market segment. The company audit assesses the company's capability to manage the threats and take advantage of the opportunities.

The search for competitive advantage

We need to convince ourselves that going to the trouble of understanding what a competitive advantage is *and* undertaking the necessary analysis in order to identify it, is actually *worthwhile*. It is worth reminding ourselves of one of the most important general points about marketing planning:

> If you cannot act on the information that you are including in the plan, do not bother to include it!

Identifying and using competitive advantage is fundamental to understanding *where* we will be getting our business from, and *how much* of it we will be getting, over the coming year.

For instance:

- If we project an increase in sales, *why will we be getting that increase?*
- If we project a decrease in sales, *why is this so?*
- If we forecast stagnant sales, *why is this?*

The increase in sales will take place either because there is a growth in the size of the market sector or because the product is taking market share away from its competitors. In either event, *the product does not have a 'natural' monopoly in any market segment* – there is always an alternative product that the consumer can use as a substitute for yours.

Why is it that the consumer chooses or rejects a product? What makes the consumer reject the competitive product or, alternatively, select the competitive product in preference to yours?

What makes the difference? The difference is competitive advantage!

There are *four* very important factors to bear in mind when we are looking at competitive advantage:

1. *Competitive advantage is a relative concept:* if the Product did have a 'natural' monopoly, there would be no competitors and everyone would use your product no matter what. Competitive advantage would not be an issue in this case. Competitive advantage has to be measured in relation to the competition (and that means identifying the competition!).
2. *Competitive advantage must be considered on a segment by segment basis:* competitors will differ from segment to segment and so will the sources of competitive advantage.
3. *A company's source of competitive advantage is likely to alter from year to year:* the most desirable source of competitive advantage is one that is sustainable. However, if your competitors are doing their marketing analysis correctly, they will be identifying your source of competitive advantage and taking steps to counterbalance it with their own.
4. *Competitive advantage is only an advantage if it adds value to your customer:* this may seem obvious, but later we shall look at examples where companies think that they have identified a competitive advantage but, in truth, it does very little to add value!

The product audit

Where will we use the information generated by undertaking this analysis? From this analysis we will understand the product-related strengths and weaknesses. This will help in the consideration of the strategic options. For example, it would be unlikely that the product would be positioned in a segment in which it did not meet the customer needs, however attractive the segment might be. This analysis also provides us with the information we need to identify how we might differentiate the product. Possible product development strategies and communication issues will also be highlighted by undertaking this analysis.

PRODUCT POSITIONING ANALYSIS

One of the techniques used to discover how well the features of our product meet the needs of each market through the benefits it can provide is the *product positioning analysis*. A major objective for product positioning analysis is to discover how well your product is 'perceived' to meet the needs of each market segment in relation to the competition. Thus, the product strengths are needs which are perceived to be satisfied by our product to a greater extent than they are perceived to be satisfied by the other products competing in the segment.

A product weakness is a need which is either:

- to be perceived to be poorly satisfied by our product; or
- to be perceived to be less well satisfied by our product than it is by competitor products.

It is important that we measure customer perception, as their perception is the 'reality' that we are trying to manage.

HOW TO UNDERTAKE A PRODUCT POSITIONING AUDIT

1. Refer back to the needs that were discovered in the segmentation process.
2. For each segment establish the priority of these needs.
3. Brief customers on the segment description. Then ask them to rank your product according to their belief as to how well it satisfies the needs.
4. Ask the same question about the leading competitor products in that segment.
5. Collect the answers from the customer and combine on a chart (Figure 9).

INTERPRETING THE INFORMATION

- Where the customer believes your product to be relatively weak, but you can prove that it is strong, you have an area which you can exploit through promotion to improve your position.
- Where there are needs that are perceived not to be well met by either you or your competitors, there might an opportunity for product development.
- Needs which your product is perceived to satisfy better than the competitors can be considered as a means of differentiating the product.
- Needs which the competitors are perceived to satisfy better than your product represent an issue. That is, if this situation is not addressed, it will affect your ability to compete.
- If all the customers' needs are satisfied very well by the majority of products in the marketplace, one can assume that these are no longer needs but, rather, customer expectations. That is, they would not expect a product to be introduced or extensively used if it did not meet these requirements. In this situation, there is a requirement to drill further down to uncover *real needs*.

Now that you have built up a clear picture of how your product fulfils the needs of the customers in a competitive sense, what are the implications of this analysis? Remember

Segment Description	Rating Scale				
Customer Needs	−1	0	1	2	3
To prevent long-term consequences				●	☆
To relieve pain		☆	●		
To increase chance that patient will find the medicine acceptable			●	☆	
To reduce likelihood that patient will forget to take medicine			●☆		

● – Competitor Products   ☆ – Our Product

FIGURE 9   THE PRODUCT POSITIONING ANALYSIS (AN EXAMPLE)

that the needs at the top of the table are the most important.

PERCEPTUAL MAPS

Another technique for expressing customer perception of your product and those with whom you compete is to produce a perceptual map to represent the positions of competitive products on a set of comparative dimensions. Figure 10 shows an example of a perceptual map for OTC analgesics.

The two dimensions here are effectiveness and gentleness. These two dimensions were selected after market research showed that they were key factors in the selection process of purchasing. 'Excedrin' is perceived as the most effective compared with other brands. If a product could be offered that combined the effectiveness of 'Excedrin' with the gentleness of Tylenol, then a strong product positioning could be achieved. It is important to repeat here that the comparative positions of products on such a map must be the result of market research findings, and not of the product manager's impressions or intuition as to how brands are likely to be perceived.

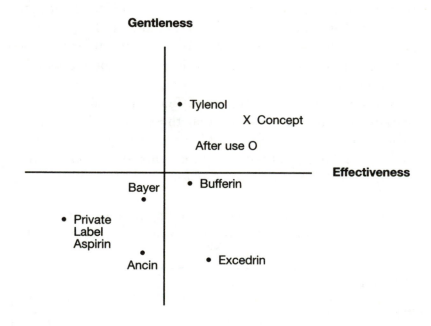

(Source: Glen L. Urban/John R. Hauser, *Design and Marketing of new Products* (1980). Reprinted by permission of Prentice-Hall.)

FIGURE 10   A PERCEPTUAL MAP FOR OTC ANALGESICS

POSITIONING PARAMETERS

Consumer products can be positioned along two dimensions:

- Price versus quality (performance).
- Price versus service.

Pharmaceutical products can be positioned and measured against a number of parameters, for example:

- Dosage, convenience.
- Efficacy versus safety.
- Price versus severity of medical condition.
- Speed and duration of action.
- Side-effect profile versus efficacy.
- Packaging convenience.
- Range, availability.

The company audit

WHERE WILL WE USE THE INFORMATION GENERATED BY UNDERTAKING THIS ANALYSIS? FROM THIS ANALYSIS WE WILL UNDERSTAND THE COMPANY-RELATED STRENGTHS AND WEAKNESSES. THIS WILL HELP US, ALONG WITH OUR UNDERSTANDING OF THE PRODUCT-RELATED STRENGTHS AND WEAKNESSES, IN GENERATING THE STRATEGIC OPTIONS. THIS ANALYSIS ALSO PROVIDES US WITH THE INFORMATION WE NEED TO IDENTIFY HOW WE MIGHT ACHIEVE COMPETITIVE ADVANTAGE.

Factors outside of the products' ability to satisfy customer needs will also affect the company's ability to compete in the future. Consequently, there is a need to explore this area too, for sources of competitive advantage.

At this point we have identified potentially profitable opportunities and market threats, so that the questions that need to be answered are:

1. Can we influence the threat(s)?
    - If yes, what do we need to have in place to enable us to do so?
    - If not, what do we need to have in place to protect our business from the threat?
2. Which are the priority opportunities?
3. What do we need to excel at to take advantage of these opportunities?

Capabilities within the company's control will be required to exploit the market segment opportunities and manage the threats. The skill is in identifying the distinctive capability(ies) – that is, a capability which the competitors lack and cannot easily reproduce, that is required to take advantage of the opportunities and manage the threats.

Distinctive capability is one route for achieving competitive advantage, but a different and equally effective route is holding a strategic asset. For example, an exclusive right to supply could be the strategic asset.

HOW TO UNDERTAKE A COMPANY AUDIT

1. Refer to the list of opportunities and threats that you have identified. Select no more than six opportunities and/or threats.
2. Brainstorm a list of capabilities that could help you to take advantage of the opportunities and/or manage the threats. Table 6 provides a general list of items that could be considered. The challenge is to identify capabilities which the competitors

lack and cannot easily reproduce, and to focus on the potential 'causes' of success rather than activities or results.

3. Having generated the ideas for distinctive capabilities, review these ideas. Some ideas may reflect a common theme. Link these together.

4. Now develop the final list. As a guideline anything that is a *must* (i.e. you cannot manage the opportunity or threat without this capability) should appear on the final list. Capabilities that help you compete for a number of the opportunities or help you manage more than one threat should also appear on the final list.

5. When you have agreed on your final list, you should then rate-weight the list by segment, and then rate your company's position within each segment as follows:
   - −1 – Really poor. Needs considerable attention.
   - 0 – Does not meet the segment requirement. Causes a few problems. Could be better.
   - 1 – Average.
   - 2 – Good. Meets the segment requirement. There is still room for improvement.
   - 3 – Excellent. Could not be better.

6. Now rate the competitors' position within each segment using the same. Remember to consider only the 'key competitors' that were identified in the market analysis and those that you have assumed will enter the segment within the planning timescale. The competitor companies should be the same ones that you considered in the product audit.

7. Combine the answers on a chart (see Table 7).

8. Note that the capabilities that are assessed will appear as the same list in each segment. The weighting of each capability, however, may differ by segment and your competitive position against each capability is likely to differ. This is because:
   - the segment requirement for the capability is different;
   - your investment across different segments is different;
   - the competition you are facing in each segment is different.

INTERPRETING THE INFORMATION

- Where your position in relation to one of the capabilities is weak relative to the competitors, you can choose to invest heavily to improve your position.
- Where there are capabilities which are not satisfied either by you or your competitors, investment in this capability might provide an opportunity for competitive advantage.
- Where your position in relation to one of the capabilities is strong relative to the competitors, you might want to think about how you can sustain this advantage.
- If the majority of competitors score 'excellent' or 'very good' in relation to a capability, it is likely that this capability is no longer a source of advantage – unless, of course, you can think of a way of doing things differently which could then create the advantage.

Before you can take advantage of your strengths, you must act to reduce your weaknesses. You also need to consider the cost of doing so. What actions and what costs are involved in converting a weakness into a strength?

TABLE 6   CAPABILITIES THAT MIGHT PROVIDE A SOURCE OF COMPETITIVE ADVANTAGE

AREA OF BUSINESS	OPPORTUNITIES	THREATS
Marketing		
Share of market	....	....
Product quality	....	....
Prices	....	....
Product acceptance	....	....
Product awareness	....	....
Advertising effectiveness	....	....
Advertising agency	....	....
Sales management	....	....
Salespeople	....	....
Customer service	....	....
Distribution capability	....	....
Customer base	....	....
Selling expenses	....	....
Distribution costs	....	....
Information	....	....
Planning capability	....	....
Other marketing items		
....	....	....
....	....	....
....	....	....
....	....	....
Production		
Plant location	....	....

TABLE 6 CONTINUED

	OPPORTUNITIES	THREATS
Capacity	....	....
Plant age	....	....
Equipment age	....	....
Quality control	....	....
Material supply	....	....
Production process	....	....
Late shipments	....	....
Expansion	....	....
Hourly labour	....	....
Supervisors	....	....
Labour availability	....	....
Union relations	....	....
Accident rate	....	....
Inventory control	....	....
Other production items		
....	....	....
....	....	....
....	....	....
....	....	....
Finance		
Profits	....	....
Cash flow	....	....
Debt–equity ratio	....	....
Dividends	....	....
Bad debts	....	....
Assets	....	....

TABLE 6   CONTINUED

	OPPORTUNITIES	THREATS
Stockholders' equity	....	....
Net income as % of sales	....	....
Earnings per share	....	....
Sales per employee	....	....
Assets per employee	....	....
Bank relations	....	....
Liquidity	....	....
Inventory management	....	....
Other finance items	....	....
....	....	....
....	....	....
....	....	....
....	....	....
Research & Development	....	....
Patents	....	....
Engineering capability	....	....
State of technology	....	....
New product success	....	....
Ability to meet timetables	....	....
Ability to meet budgets	....	....
Breadth of expertise	....	....
Other R & D items	....	....
....	....	....
....	....	....
....	....	....
....	....	....

TABLE 6   CONCLUDED

	OPPORTUNITIES	THREATS
Management	....	....
Turnover		
Experience		
Communications		
Reporting responsibilities	....	....
Ability to meet plans	....	....
Decisiveness of decisions		
Compatibility		
Depth of talent	....	....
Other management items		
....	....	....
....	....	....
....	....	....
....	....	....

TABLE 7   EXAMPLE COMPANY AUDIT

Segment Description: Required Company Capabilities	Weighting	Rating Scale				
		−1	0	1	2	3
Brand awareness						
Product differentiation						
Sales force size						
Distribution, etc.						
	100					

Interpreting strengths and weaknesses

WHERE WILL WE USE THE INFORMATION GENERATED BY DRAWING THESE CONCLUSIONS? IN TWO PLACES. OUR UNDERSTANDING OF OUR COMPETITIVE POSITION WILL BE USED TO HELP US IDENTIFY THE STRATEGIC OPTIONS. ALSO, ONCE WE HAVE DECIDED ON A PRODUCT STRATEGY, IT IS FROM THESE CONCLUSIONS THAT WE WILL DETERMINE WHAT IS CRITICAL TO SUCCESS.

What is a strength? A strength is any market requirement that we can satisfy better than our competitors.

What is a weakness? A weakness is a market requirement which we are unable to satisfy or satisfy less well than our competitors.

Strengths and weakness are likely to be segment-specific. They must be understood for realistic future strategies and objectives to be constructed and understood.

While most companies understand how their product helps them compete, it is surprising how few product managers ever honestly examine their strengths or appraise their weaknesses, let alone interrelate the two and interrelate them with their understanding of the market opportunities and threats. Yet, without this balance of judgment, one can never fully exploit the opportunities.

4

The SWOT Analysis

What is a SWOT analysis?

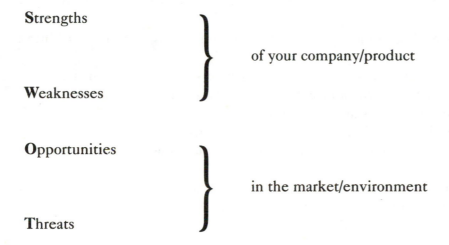

Strengths

Weaknesses

} of your company/product

Opportunities

Threats

} in the market/environment

Often also referred to as the OTSW analysis. It is a method for integrating and cross-analysing all the data you have collected in the market audit, environmental audit, product audit and company audit. It helps you in two ways:

1. *To identify the priority market segments*. The priority is determined by the segment's overall attractiveness. An attractive segment is likely to be one which presents a lot of opportunity and in which you are competitive for this opportunity. However, it could also be one where you are confident of your ability to create the opportunity and/or improve your position to become competitive for the opportunity.
2. *To identify the priority opportunities*. That is, it also helps you identify, within the segment, those opportunities which are best for the company and your product because you either have, or can acquire, the strengths to take advantage of them.

Why do you need a SWOT analysis?

In the market and environmental audits you will have identified several market segments which are potentially viable for your product. From the company audit you know the major strengths and weaknesses of the company. In your product audit you have established the actual position of your product in each segment. This combination of information tells you where you are, and provides the basis, therefore, for understanding where you might get to (in sales terms).

You now need:

1. to arrive at a way of getting there (also commonly referred to as a 'strategy');
2. to decide on the specific things you need to do to make this happen. These are commonly referred to as 'tactics'.

SWOT analysis is a technique that combines all the information from the different audits to help you arrive at a decision on the above. In particular, it is a method designed to help produce:

- the optimum segment to attack and the reasons why (i.e. the positioning of the product);
- the 'message' to communicate and the reasons 'why' (i.e. how to differentiate the product);
- the 'target audience' and why (i.e. the people who need to hear this message);
- as a combination of the above, the strategy that will bring success;
- the tactical objectives and their priority;
- a tactical plan that will meet the tactical objectives and product goals;
- a final check that you have carried out a complete market and product review.

The situational analysis is your presentation of this information in the narrative which helps the reader understand the issues and, therefore, puts into context the options that you have gone on to consider.

How to build a SWOT analysis

The SWOT analysis considers the aspects of marketing beyond just market share and market growth, important though they are.

STEP 1 – OPPORTUNITIES AND THREATS

These come out of the following areas:

- Market segment.
- Market analysis.
- Environmental analysis.

The first step is to identify those factors from the environmental and market audits which have either positive or negative implications for your company and your products (e.g. a decline in the size of a segment, new technologies being developed, etc.). You should identify only those key factors which affect your potential segments in a positive or negative manner. Once you have done this, rewrite the negative factors in a positive manner: for example, a high level of price sensitivity becomes a low level of price sensitivity. Thus, if a factor does not appear in one segment, it will automatically become a threat or an opportunity when you do the analysis: for example, if 'weak competition' as a factor is considered to be important for your product to be successful and it does not exist in a segment, you have a threat.

There is no 'perfect' list that would suit every product in every segment. Below are some examples of the types of factor that have proved useful.

EXAMPLE LIST OF OPPORTUNITIES

In the market

- Large segment size

- High growth rate due to increased level of diagnosis

- High level of customer interest

- High degree of acceptance

- Many new customers

- Low level of price-sensitivity

- Unmet need

- High level of dissatisfaction

- Reimbursement status

In the environment

- Few government regulations

- Little negative public opinion

- Growth economy

- Competition:

    - few competitors

    - weak selling power

    - no new products

    - poor marketing skills

    - few financial resources

    - little promotion activity

    - poor image

    - large product range

Having considered these factors, produce a list, based on your earlier analysis, which represents the absolute key items. You should aim to finish with about 10 or 12 factors. If it is longer than this, it will be difficult to work with and probably reflects a lack of hard thinking about the market in which you wish to be, or are, operating.

STEP 2 – STRENGTHS AND WEAKNESSES

These always come from *within* – that is, from the product itself or from the company. The second step is to construct a list in exactly the same way as you did for opportunities and threats. Strengths and weaknesses come from the company audit and from the product audit. From these audits look for instances where you are above or below average. It is in these instances where you have particular strengths and weaknesses.

Again, rewrite weaknesses as strengths: for example, poor technical support becomes excellent technical support. See the list below for examples:

EXAMPLES OF STRENGTHS

Product

- Highly efficient product

- Very reliable

- Convenient packaging

- Acceptable pricing

- Excellent technical back-up

- High versatility

- High market segment share

- Good trade mark

- Excellent delivery

Company

- Large sales force

- Excellent reputation

- Adequate promotion budgets

- Productive R & D

- Well-motivated sales force

- Effective sales force

- Well-trained sales force

- Excellent distribution

- Excellent back-up information

Again, using the information generated in your earlier analysis, you should edit it down to those items which are important to the market. Remember that we cannot ignore a weakness just because we know we cannot satisfy it, if it is a factor judged essential.

STEP 3 – WEIGHTING THE LISTS

You now have two lists of factors against which you will wish to measure the various potential segments. However, the lists are in random order and cannot be cross-analysed. A moment's thought will show you that in any list all the factors are not equal. Some will be more important than others. This is a decision area for you. *Put the lists in order of importance* so that the most important factor is at the top, and the least important at the bottom. Now you need to decide how much more important one factor is than another. *Allocate 100 points across the factors to represent this relative importance.* Table 8 is an example of how this can be done. You have now weighted the list and can move from your judgment and belief to considering *reality*. (*Note*: the weightings applied to the opportunity and threat criteria should be consistent for each segment.) However, the weighting applied to the strength/weakness criteria will be segment-specific.

TABLE 8 SWOT ANALYSIS

Opportunities and Threats	Weight	Segment 1 Rating	Segment 1 Score	Segment 2 Rating	Segment 2 Score	Segment 3 Rating	Segment 3 Score	Segment 4 Rating	Segment 4 Score
High level of customer dissatisfaction	19	1	19	3	57	2	38	-1	-19
Number of patients	15	1	15	2	30	-1	-15	2	30
% drug treated	15	2	30	3	45	3	45	3	45
Willingness to prescribe expensive treatments	15	2	30	2	30	3	45	1	15
High level of patient/carer expectations	8	2	16	2	16	0	0	0	0
Limited customer habit	8	0	0	2	16	-1	-8	0	0
Move to community care	4	3	12	0	0	-1	-4	3	12
Patient advocacy group pressure	4	2	8	1	4	0	0	-1	-4
Level of competitor activity	4	-1	-4	0	0	2	8	2	8
Size of customer base	4	2	8	1	4	3	12	0	0
High cost to society	4	0	0	3	12	3	12	-1	-4
Total	100		134		214		133		83

Strengths and Weaknesses	Segment 1 Weight	Segment 1 Rating	Segment 1 Score	Segment 2 Weight	Segment 2 Rating	Segment 2 Score	Segment 3 Weight	Segment 3 Rating	Segment 3 Score	Segment 4 Weight	Segment 4 Rating	Segment 4 Score
Differentiation	18	1	18	18	0	0	18	0	0	12	-1	-12
Data/evidence	12	1	12	8	0	0	18	0	0	4	0	0
Experience	12	0	0	18	0	0	18	1	18	12	-1	-12
Targeting	5	2	10	12	2	24	18	1	18	12	2	24
Endorsement	15	2	30	8	2	16	8	1	8	18	0	0
Positioning	18	2	36	12	2	24	8	0	0	12	0	0
Skilled Sales force	12	3	36	12	2	24	8	1	8	12	2	24
Education	8	1	8	12	1	12	4	1	4	18	1	18
Total	100		150	100		100	100		56	100		42

STEP 4 – SCORING

SCORING SCALE: OPPORTUNITY

Score	Criteria
3	Most attractive segment. Very good.
2	Better than most. Above average. Good.
1	Average. OK.
0	Below average. Not good enough.
–1	Among the worst. Really poor.

SCORING SCALE: COMPETITIVE POSITION

Score	Criteria
3	Best in segment. Maximum. Clearly the leader. Top quality.
2	Above average. Better than most. Good quality.
1	Average. Not a current problem. OK.
0	Causes some problems. Could be better. Not improving.
–1	Among the worst. Always a problem. Really bad. Needs a lot of attention.

Now you will need to give points to each element that you listed, refer to the scales above. There are several vital things to remember:

- *Opportunities* can exist now or appear during the planned period. For example, a new competitor might be expected within six months. This should not be ignored just because it does not exist today. Thus for *opportunities and threats we are concerned with the present position, trends and future expectations.*
- *Strengths and weaknesses*, on the other hand, *exist now*. Do not anticipate a successful change. For example, you could have a sales force which you want to direct into a new area. Currently, you would have a problem with training, experience and familiarization. Because you could rectify this with a training programme, do not assume success. Wait until the successful results are achieved before you alter the scoring.
- *For evaluating all of the factors*, we are interested in *reality*, not the internal company views and opinions. For example, you might have a 60-strong sales force, which is considered large by company standards. However, if your competitors in that segment also have a 60-strong sales force, then you are only average.

● Similarly, wherever possible you are interested in *the reality of your target audience's attitudes and perceptions*. Product managers, and chief executives quite naturally believe their products are better than the competition, and may even have data to prove it. However, if doctors believe that all the products in that area have equal effectiveness, then the company opinion is not only commercially worthless but has an inherent danger of misdirecting activities and raising false expectations. Scores should reflect facts as perceived in the marketplace.

So, bearing these points in mind, refer to research results and your earlier analysis and apply the scoring scale shown in Table 8. Remember, use facts wherever possible; try to avoid assumptions.

STEP 5 – RANKING

If you multiply the score by the weight, you will end up with a ranking for every segment by factor: by threats and opportunities and by strengths and weaknesses.

STEP 6 – DECISION PROCESS

The worked example contains four segments. To select the most immediate and best strategy, you can use the grid shown in Figure 11 to see graphically where each of your segments falls depending on its total score on each of the axes: opportunities, threats, strengths and weaknesses.

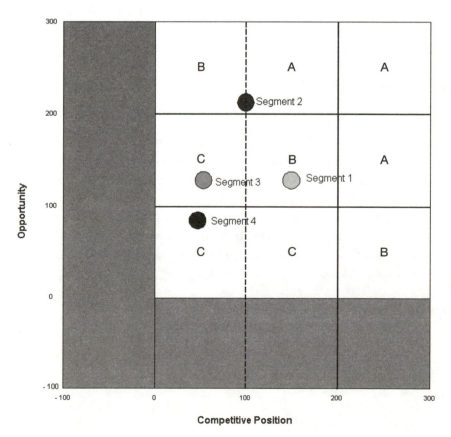

FIGURE 11 THE STRATEGIC DECISION GRID

Your selection of the best segment to attack is dependent upon where it falls in the grid (square A, B or C).

- Squares marked C are high-risk with a high probability of failure, since either opportunities or strengths (or both) are below 100.
- Squares marked B show, potentially a more successful situation, as either opportunities or strengths are very high, or are both average and well balanced.
- Squares marked A are the *target areas*. High in opportunities and strengths.

In the worked example Segment 4 falls in C, and, arguably, does not warrant further investigation. Segments 2 and 3 fall in B and Segment 1 falls in A.

Assuming these are the choices available, your immediate decision might be to concentrate on Segments 1, 2 and 3. However, before you make any decisions you need to consider the information underlying the picture. What are the issues that would need to be managed in Segments 1, 2 and 3?

Considering the information as it is presented to you in Figure 12 enables you to identify whether there might be any threats which you could influence, i.e. create opportunity. Also, at this point you would need to identify the capabilities that would be required to influence these threats, and take a view as to how easy it will be for you to acquire these capabilities, if you do not already possess them.

The final stage in identifying the issues relates to the opportunities that exist in each segment. You need to establish whether there are opportunities for which you are currently not competitive. If yes, can you become competitive? How quickly can you become competitive? See Table 9 on page 58.

STEP 7 – DEVELOPING A STRATEGY

Given the results in this example, the strategies could be:

- to promote product *x* in Segments 1 and 2, emphasizing whatever the basis for the differentiation is. Action would also be taken to create additional opportunity in Segment 1 through influencing customer habit. Our intention would be to pick up the lion's share of this opportunity;
- to aggressively promote Product *x* in Segment 2 only, emphasizing whatever the basis for the differentiation is. It is also clear that action would be taken to address the customer's experience and generate the necessary data/evidence which affects our competitiveness.

STEP 8 – DEVELOPING MARKETING OBJECTIVES

Given these strategies, what tactical change must we achieve? Once again, a study of the ranking establishes what we must achieve, and, because of the segment-specific weighting, the order of importance.

Segment 1

Opportunities	**Threats**
% drug treated	Customer habit
Willingness to prescribe	Level of competitor activity
expensive treatments	Cost to society
High level of patient/carer	
expectations	
Move to community care	
Patient advocacy group pressure	
Size of customer base	

Strengths	**Weaknesses**
Targeting	Experience
Endorsement	
Positioning	
Skilled salesforce	

Segment 2

Opportunities	**Threats**
High level of customer dissatisfaction	Level of competitor activity
Number of patients	High cost to society
% drug treated	
Willingness to prescribe expensive treatments	
High level of patient/carer expectations	
Limited customer habit	
Move to community care	
Patient advocacy group pressure	
Size of customer base	

Strengths	**Weaknesses**
Targeting	Differentiation
Endorsement	Data/evidence
Positioning	Experience
Skilled Salesforce	

Segment 3

Opportunities	**Threats**
High level of customer dissatisfaction	Number of patients
% drug treated	High level of patient/carer expectations
Willingness to prescribe expensive treatments	Limited customer habit
Size of customer base	Move to community care
Level of competitor activity	Patient advocacy group pressure
High cost to society	

Strengths	**Weaknesses**
	Differentiation
	Data/evidence
	Positioning

FIGURE 12 THE TRADITIONAL SWOT

TABLE 9   INTERPRETATION OF THE ISSUES

Segment 1	Segment 2
Willingness to prescribe expensive treatments (o)	High level of customer dissatisfaction (o)
Skilled sales force (s)	Differentiation (w)
Positioning (s)	Positioning (s)
Targeting (s)	Endorsement (s)
Customer habit (t)	Level of competitor activity (t)
Experience (w)	Differentiation (w)
Targeting (s)	Experience (w)
Endorsement (s)	Positioning (s)
	Targeting (s)

1. *Strategy A: CSFs and objectives*:
   - *Differentiation:* Within six months to ensure that 60 per cent of all customers are convinced that Product x is more effective than the competition. Within one year to have 60 per cent of customers willing to prescribe Product x in both Segments 1 and 2.
   - *Positioning:* 80 per cent of customers within a month of launch will position Product x (unprompted) in line with our strategy.
   - *Endorsement:* Nine out of twelve opinion leaders will be prepared to present Product x favourably at meetings.
   - *Experience:* 25 per cent of customers (i.e. the target customers) will have treated a minimum of three patients with Product x within four months of the product launch.
2. *Strategy B: CSFs and objectives*:
   - *Differentiation:* Within six months to ensure that 60 per cent of all customers are convinced that Product x is more effective than the competition.
   - *Experience:* 50 per cent of customers (i.e. the target customers) will have treated a minimum of three patients with Product x within four months of the product launch.
   - *Targeting:* At launch all customers will have been profiled by the sales force as 'high potential, medium potential and low potential'. This profiling will also have been validated by independent research.

CONCLUSION

The quantified SWOT analysis described in this chapter is one of your most valuable marketing planning tools. It gives you and your marketing colleagues a mechanism to arrive at a number of marketing decisions. Setting up the initial data for a SWOT analysis takes time, but, provided you do it on a computer, then the greater part of the work is done. Thereafter, when you need to update the model or to input some new information so that you can assess the knock-on effects on all the other marketing variables, the task is much easier to complete. And, in marketing, time is always in short supply.

From the worked examples, you can see how the SWOT analysis can help you decide upon the best course of action, even though there is a multiplicity of factors involved. The more effort, thinking and judgment you put into this task, the better the results will be. Remember that one person's list provides the other person's questions. Always know the reasons for your priority and weighting decisions. If you cannot justify the lists, why should anyone else accept them? For the scoring use facts, even though they may be unpalatable. If the factor is significantly 'political', scoring high will only result in failures as time goes on. Identification of weaknesses, on the other hand, will allow steps to be taken to improve future performance. There is one way to ensure that factual and honest contributions are made by those who take part in your company's SWOT analysis workshop, which should be the starting point of your planning process. The most senior people present should always kick off the discussion about the company's weaknesses by stating what theirs are. Others will then be much more willing to do the same. For marketing planning, facts are a much more sound foundation upon which to build the future than dreams.

5

Product Strategy

Introduction

In the reference to the marketing planning process in Chapter 1 we said planning involved answering four questions, one of which is: 'How will we get there?' There are many ways to find answers to this question.

> The problem is that most managers prefer to sell the products they find easiest to sell to those customers who offer the least line of resistance. By developing short-term, tactical marketing plans first and then extrapolating them, managers merely succeed in extrapolating their own short-comings. ('Ten barriers to marketing planning'. Malcolm McDonald. *Journal of marketing management*, 1989, 3).

Good planning demands that logical alternatives are explored. These alternatives are referred to as strategies.

Definition of terms used

It is easy to get bogged down in terminology, but there are some terms which define exactly what it is that we are trying to do, and thus it is essential that everybody has the same understanding of what these terms really mean.

First let us be clear what the words 'objective', 'strategy' and 'tactics' mean. Table 10 gives their meanings and implications.

STRATEGY

When we refer to strategy, we are talking about a game plan. It is a broad statement describing how we intend to achieve the financial objectives (product goals) set out in the marketing plan. Each objective can be achieved in a number of ways.

For example, the objective *increase volume of sales by 4 per cent* can be achieved by:

(a) increasing sales in a particular segment (either by growing the segment or taking share from the competition);
(b) penetrating a completely new segment (either by promoting the product on its existing attributes or by repositioning the product for that segment).

(a) and (b) are different strategies.

TABLE 10   DEFINITION OF TERMS USED

CONCEPTS	ILLUSTRATIONS	CONTENTS
Objectives	Destination	What you need to achieve. Which must be: ● quantified ● measurable ● desirable ● realistic
Strategies	Road	A description of how you intend to achieve your objective: ● target audience ● key product features/ benefits you will stress ● the segment(s) you will attack
Tactics	Vehicle	A description of the actions you will take or the methods you will use to achieve the strategy, i.e. promotion policy.

A strategy defines the route selected from a number of choices that are available. A strategy enables you to:

● integrate all the elements of the business that are required for the product to be marketed successfully;
● direct the allocation of resources and effort required;
● be selective as to the means of achieving the goals.

OBJECTIVES

Objectives should be set at every level of business: financial, marketing, product, sales, production, distribution. There are:

● *company objectives*, which specify the company's financial goals and mission;

- *marketing objectives*, which specify the way these goals will be achieved;
- *product objectives*, which specify the performance goals of a product. Chapter 7 covers this in depth. Basically, these are your sales and market share target for the year – for example, sales of $5.2 million and a share of 12.7 per cent.

It is worth repeating here what has already been said about objectives. All business objectives set for your product should be:

S pecific

M easurable

A mbitious

R ealistic

T imed

TACTICS

If the strategy represents the broad marketing thrusts that the manager will use to achieve the financial objectives (product goals), each element of the marketing strategy must be elaborated to answer: *what* will be done? *when* will it be done? *who* will do it? *how much* will it cost? These are the tactics.

Tactics define and spell out in detail the specific activities that must be carried out to reach the stated objectives. These tactical activities will be described in detail in Chapter 7, 'Promotion'. In this chapter we will show how tactics must follow from your strategy statements.

The tactics allow the *implementation* of the marketing strategy to take place. Implementing the plan is the most visible part of the job. However, devising a workable strategy in order to achieve realistic objectives is an equally important part of marketing planning.

Generating the strategic options

After a company has evaluated different segments, it must decide which and how many segments to serve. Before you write down a final strategy statement for your product, you need to understand the choices that are open to you.

Various individuals and organizations have come up with lists of possible strategies which companies could pursue.

THE ANSOFF MATRIX

One early list was proposed by Ansoff (*Corporate Strategy*, revised edition, New York, McGraw-Hill, 1987), who identified market penetration, product development, market development and diversification as alternative strategic objectives (see Figure 13).

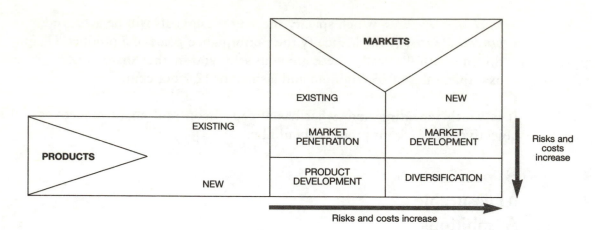

FIGURE 13   THE ANSOFF MATRIX

MARKET PENETRATION STRATEGY

This strategy consists of seeking to *increase* sales and *market share* in *existing markets* from *current product(s)* through a series of more aggressive marketing activities that encourages greater usage.

Tactics – for example:

- Increasing sales activities to obtain more market share by doubling the sales force call-frequency on A-class doctors.
- Increasing brand awareness of a new product, by organizing more doctors' meetings with key specialists.
- Introducing an initial sale-or-return policy for all pharmacies in Month 1 on OTC product to obtain its correct shelf space to correspond with its brand share.

The most important point to remember about a market penetration strategy is that, unless you plan to do something *different, more aggressive* and *more innovative* than last year, there is no real reason or likelihood that you will sell the same amount of product next year, let alone achieve an increase.

PRODUCT DEVELOPMENT STRATEGY

This strategy consists of seeking to increase sales by developing either *new* or *improved* products for an existing market segment in which your company is well established.

Tactics – for example:

- Developing new product features which will enable you to offer new benefits, or minimize or eradicate existing product problems.
- Creating a higher-quality version of an existing product to increase usage of the product.
- Offering better value for money by, for example, modifying pack sizes.

MARKET DEVELOPMENT STRATEGY

This strategy consists of seeking increased sales by taking current products into a new market or market segment. Pharmaceutical products can be developed to the point where they are safe enough to move from the prescription to the proprietary/OTC market. New indications, enabling a drug to be prescribed for a totally different group of patients from the one for which the drug was originally developed, is a perfect example of market development strategy.

Tactics – for example:

● Promoting a pharmaceutical drug to a group of specialists (dermatologists) to whom the product was not promoted before.

DIVERSIFICATION

This strategy is the most *risky* and *costly*: entering a new market with a completely new product. A decision to do this usually stems from the lack of any real additional growth or profit opportunities resulting from exploiting the three strategic options already described. When identifying new market opportunities, you should always look for those that enable you to *exploit corporate strengths*. Diversification at the product level is rare.

THE BOSTON CONSULTING GROUP

Alternative strategies are:

● invest;
● hold;
● harvest;
● divest.

Refer to the BCG grid in Chapter 2.

MICHAEL PORTER (COMPETITIVE STRATEGY, 1980)

Porter put forward the view that there are two dimensions of choice in business strategy. Firms can pursue either cost leadership – the same product as competitors but at lower cost – or differentiation (see Figure 14).

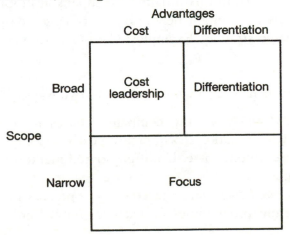

FIGURE 14 PORTER'S COMPETITIVE STRATEGY MODEL

The company can also consider strategy in terms of how it chooses to approach the market; that is, it can adopt a global approach or be more selective in the approach to the various segments. For example:

- *Single Segment Concentration*: this is the simplest strategy, i.e. the company concentrates all its efforts and resources on a single segment, e.g. Rolex watches – the premium, luxury watch segment.

  Through concentrated marketing the company achieves a strong position in the segment – it develops a solid knowledge of the segment and builds a strong reputation – the potential for a positive return on investment is high, but the company has 'all its eggs' in one basket.

  This can be dangerous if the need for the company's product is satisfied in a new and different way (e.g. the slide rule is replaced by the calculator), by a new competitor or one who enters the market with a similar product perceived to offer 'better value for money'.

- *Selective Specialization*: in this situation the company selects a number of segments, each of which is attractive and fits the company's objectives and resources. There may be little or no synergy between the segments.

  This strategy of *multi-segment* coverage has the advantage over *single-segment* concentration of diversifying the company's risk, but the disadvantages of limited economies of scale.

- *Product Specialization*: in this situation the company concentrates on making a certain product and sells it to a number of different segments: e.g. a microscope manufacturer may sell microscopes to schools, universities, forensic depts, etc. The microscopes will be different for each group, but the company does not make anything other than microscopes.

  Through this strategy the company builds up a strong reputation in a specific product area, but there is an associated risk if the product is replaced through entirely different technology.

- *Market Specialization*: here a company concentrates on serving many needs of any particular segment. Example: A range of products for school laboratories – microscopes, bunsen burners, glass tubes.

  The advantage is that the company becomes known as a specialist supplier for that particular customer group and is the natural supplier, *but* what happens if schools have their budgets cut by government?

- *Full Market Coverage*: in this situation a company attempts to serve all segments with all the products they might need. Only very large companies can undertake a 'full market' coverage strategy. Examples: Coca-Cola (beverage market), Ford (transport market).

Large companies can cover a whole market in two ways:

1. *Undifferentiated marketing*: the company ignores market segment differences and pursues the whole market. Example: the early strategy of Coca-Cola – one drink, in one size bottle, in one taste. Undifferentiated marketing is defended on grounds of cost economies.
2. *Differentiated marketing*: here the company operates in most market segments but designs different programmes for each segment. Ford offers a different vehicle for

different purposes (domestic and commercial) and personalities. Differentiated marketing typically creates more sales than undifferentiated marketing, but the costs are higher:

- production costs;
- administration costs;
- advertising and promotion costs;
- research costs, etc.

Differentiated marketing can be used by minor players in the market to gain a foothold in a particular niche, i.e. by identifying an opportunity not directly concentrated on by the market leader (e.g. Losec, Tie Rack, Eco washing-up liquid).

Selecting a strategy

To decide on your product strategy, you need to answer four questions:

1. Which segment?
2. With what intent?
3. With what message?
4. Which target audience?

WHICH SEGMENT?

To define a market segment as being attractive and worthwhile to exploit, *four* conditions must be met:

1. *Measurability*: You must be able to measure the size of the segment so that you can monitor its size and your product's performance against that of your competitors.
2. *Accessibility*: You must be able to focus company marketing resources on the chosen segment; for example, if the sales force or other promotional means cannot reach the decision-makers in that segment, the segment is not accessible.
3. *Substantiality*: The segment must be large and profitable enough to be worth exploiting. Having limited resources, one must concentrate on the segments likely to produce higher returns.
4. *Homogeneity*: The segment must have consumers/customers with sufficiently similar needs to make it suitable for your product's promotional methods to be cost-effective.

To help identify worthwhile segments, ask yourself the following questions:

- What is the segment's potential?
- Does the sales potential support the cost of promotion?
- What are the opportunities in a particular segment?
- Are you competitive for these opportunities?
- Can you identify any unsatisfied needs?
- If so, can your product satisfy them?
- Are there threats that could reduce the size of the potential, or close the window of opportunity?

- Does this segment offer you a position in the market which no one else holds?
- Could this segment offer you a position in the market which no one else holds?

WITH WHAT INTENT?

The intent should describe the very 'essence' of your strategy. For example, your intention might be to 're-engineer' the market so that the product can be used in a timely and appropriate fashion, or to 'develop the market' so that people who are not currently able to access appropriate care can do so in the future, etc. For possible strategic intent descriptors, refer back to discussion on different strategies.

WITH WHAT MESSAGE?

Having decided which segments to operate in and with which intent, you must now decide which product benefits/features you will emphasize to differentiate yourself within those segments.

WHICH TARGET AUDIENCE?

Having identified where it is you want your product used (i.e. which segment), and why you believe it should be used (i.e. the message), you now need to select the target audience – that is, the decision-makers and influencers upon which you will concentrate your marketing resources. In today's environment this is likely to include the payers, purchasers, providers and public.

Customer segmentation is a tool which can be used to influence 'how' the strategy is implemented. Customer segments do not need to vary in line with product strategy; in fact, it is better if they are independent of product strategy – that is, they should influence the way the company communicates with its customers with a view to ensuring that their communication is more effective than their competitors' communication.

Customers can be segmented according to their information needs. The types of need we are interested in might include:

- their preference for how they receive information;
- what type of information they would like to receive;
- to what extent they seek third party opinion;
- the likely source of third party opinion, etc.

A crude form of customer segmentation has always existed. For example, there has been a general belief that the type of information specialists need to receive will be different from that of general practitioners, who in turn differ in their information requirements from nurses. Today, increasingly, there is a tendency to believe that it does not matter whether we are talking to a physician, a nurse, a pharmaceutical advisor, or someone from the senior management team of the payor organization. What does matter is how we have segmented them and which segment they might fall into, as this will influence how the company approaches and communicates with them.

Thus, irrespective of product and product strategy, the implementation of that strategy might be enhanced where customer segmentation is recognized and practised.

WRITING THE PRODUCT STRATEGY STATEMENT

You should describe the precise direction you will take to achieve the stated profit contribution, marketing, sales and other objectives for your product. The statement should provide a broad outline of how you will achieve your objectives. Make the statement a practical one.

ISSUES TO CONSIDER WHEN SELECTING A STRATEGY

The actual choice of your target marketing strategy will be governed by a number of constraints, such as:

- *Company resources*: where your company resources are too limited to enable you to cover all markets (e.g. advertising budget, limited sales force size in relation to your major competitors, plant or stock capacity), it is only realistic to go for a concentrated target market.
- *Product homogeneity*: undifferentiated marketing is more appropriate for products that are so basic that they can meet a mass-market need. Throat lozenges such as Strepsils or Mac are examples. Products tailored to very specific medical conditions are more appropriate to concentrated and/or differentiated target markets.
- *Product life cycle stage*: you should examine where your product is in its life cycle. At the introduction stage your strategy may be to concentrate on a particular segment so that your product becomes first choice among doctors for a particular treatment. Alternatively, your product may be well into the mature stage of its life cycle, and you are actively broadening its position so that you can take it into different target markets.
- *Marketing homogeneity*: where consumers have the same needs or react in the same way to marketing stimuli, an undifferentiated target marketing strategy could be adopted. Some hospital products fall into this category, particularly dressings and catheters.
- *Competitive marketing*: if your competitors are concentrating on a particular market segment, you are unlikely to be able to compete successfully if you are following an undifferentiated, target-marketing strategy. This is particularly true when 'me too' products are battling it out for market and sales volume. However, if your analysis indicates that one or more competitors are operating an undifferentiated, target-marketing strategy, you can probably mount a successful strategy by concentrated marketing, dedicating all your marketing and sales resources to dominating a specific, commercially worthwhile segment with your product.

Note: All of these items will have been considered in the SWOT analysis (see Chapter 4).

6

Sales Forecasting and Strategy

Introduction

Marketing's contribution to business success lies in its commitment to detailed analysis of future opportunities to meet customer needs, and a professional approach to selling to defined market segments the products that deliver the sought after benefits. The quantification of the way this will be delivered to the customer, is the *sales forecast*.

The sales forecast is a considered estimate of the product's future performance. It is based on a set of assumptions about the market and the company/product's competitive position.

The sales forecast might be determined bottom-up or top-down. The bottom-up process relies on the product manager exploring a number of different, plausible strategies alongside a set of forecasts which can be submitted to the board for their consideration. A top-down process is one where the revenue and profit expectations are predetermined, and the role of the product manager is to identify a strategy and action plan that will deliver these numbers.

Either way there is a requirement for the product manager to be able to consider the revenue and profit implications associated with any one strategy.

This chapter provides a framework for forecasting. It considers the individual steps that form part of developing a forecast covering the planning horizon. It also recognizes that there are three different levels at which forecasting takes place:

- *Market Potential*: this refers to the upper limit of demand or the expected sales of all similar product types over a given period. In general, it will tend to be relatively stable, although climate and political decisions can have an impact. This forecast represents the ability of the market to absorb a particular type of product.
- *Sales Potential*: this is the estimate of a product's maximum sales volume over a particular period of time. It reflects the demand that would exist if maximum sales-generating activities were executed in a given time period under certain market conditions.
- *Sales Forecast*: this is the actual expected sales volume over the given period of time. It will be lower than the sales potential because the company will always be

constrained by resources, or a focus that is on achieving the highest profit, rather than maximizing volume growth.

Why forecasting is important

It is recognized universally that there is a need to form a systematic and coherent view of the future as a basis for making decisions. Yet views on organized business forecasting frequently go far beyond healthy scepticism towards an attitude of outright cynicism. So what tends to alienate the intelligent manager?

- Inaccessibility to the non-statistically initiated.
- Techniques of analysis which never bear much relation to the problems managers face.

The sales forecast involves the predicting of the product or 'family' sales over some specific time in the future. It is the foundation for the budgeting process and therefore influences much, if not all, of the Company's activities.

A good forecast helps in the planning and control of production, distribution and promotion activity. The forecast may suggest change in price structures, budgeting procedures or stockholding. Operational planning is highly dependent upon the sales forecast, therefore ensuring its accuracy remains essential.

Mistakes in forecasting can give rise to serious errors in other areas of the company, leading to loss of profitability. For example, an underestimate of sales could give rise to underproduction, leading to lost sales, while an overestimate would mean a stockpiling of raw materials or finished goods that could end up unusable or unsaleable.

The sales forecast is also a control and monitoring function, as it establishes an evaluation standard. This should be used for evaluating the successes and failures of marketing and providing 'experience' opportunities for individual improvement.

Forecasting systems are, today, designed to take much of the burden out of sales forecast generation. The time-consuming and tedious aspects of calculation and cross-relationship are performed by a computer. You are left with the more creative and significant activities of thinking and evaluation. Although a system is designed to be mostly illustrative, it is not entirely hands-off.

An important item to remember is that a computer only illustrates the result of your thoughts and decisions. It is not an intelligent beast and should never control you. The inputs are your beliefs, so if you do not agree with the predicted results challenge the beliefs. Never even think 'the computer said this, it must be so!'.

The market forecast

As we know, markets are not static, but in a constant state of change. This provides a major problem in forecasting because, typically, we depend on extending past experience into the future to develop the forecast.

For example, if there is a sudden product withdrawal which we had not anticipated, this has such an impact on the market that part of the history of demand for this and similar types of products is next to worthless. Other problems with forecasting are concerned with data: seasonality, erratic sales, or incomplete sales data.

HOW TO APPROACH THE MARKET FORECAST

The first step is to produce a mathematical forecast based upon historic sales trends. This produces a baseline which provides a perspective for your final forecast and prevents grossly distorted figures appearing. This forecast assumes that the past will continue into the future. Even allowing that the forecast will be weighted so that recent trends have more importance than previous ones, we know that the future will be different. We will be exercising our skill to improve our products' competitive strength, and presumably so will the competition. The environmental factors that drive the market will also be subject to change. Therefore, our next problem is to decide by how much our forecast will deviate from the underlying trend.

WHAT IS THE UNDERLYING TREND FORECAST?

The underlying trend forecast is the base forecast; it is a standard projection of past trends. It uses no information other than past sales data.

The underlying trend forecast will give an indication of future trends but it assumes that what went on in the past will continue in the future (as you know, this is rarely the case). However, the underlying trend forecast will be a good start.

The underlying trend forecast will include seasonality (where applicable) and trends. It will also attempt to dilute 'blips'. The underlying trend forecast will consider all past data, but puts more weight on more recent data. To get a realistic underlying trend forecast you will need *at least* $3^{1}/_{2}$ years data (to account for seasonality), which means that *this system is inappropriate for forecasting new markets*.

The underlying *volume trend forecast* should always be the starting point for forecasting. This should be done for each target market segment. Segments that are not included in the list of target market segments should be considered as 'the balance of the market'.

The next question that must be asked is: how much does the underlying trend understand about the future market environment and other influencing factors? To what extent will it consider:

- changes in the environment?
- competitors' activity?
- changes in our promotion, etc?

Your understanding of what *has been* influencing the underlying trend at a segment level was determined in your market analysis. If, in your environmental analysis, your conclusion was that the market would be subject to minor changes only, then projecting the underlying trend into the future would be an acceptable view of the shape of the future market.

This is, however, unlikely. It is more likely that you will have determined that different trends are having a greater or lesser impact on each segment.

The challenge when undertaking the market forecast is to refer back to the conclusions from your environmental analysis. Isolate those trends affecting the prescription market volume and make assumptions about the extent to which these trends will affect each market segment. In your earlier analysis you would already have decided whether the impact is positive or negative, so that it is now just a matter of quantifying the impact. In practice you might find it useful to consider the implications of the trend – for example, in Rx/physician terms – and convert this into a total market figure which then can be apportioned to the relevant segments. Table 11 gives you a framework for building this forecast.

Thus, you will end up with a future 'size' and market growth figure which has been determined by taking history into account and projecting this forward, then adjusting for the 'key changes' which you assumed would take place in your environmental analysis.

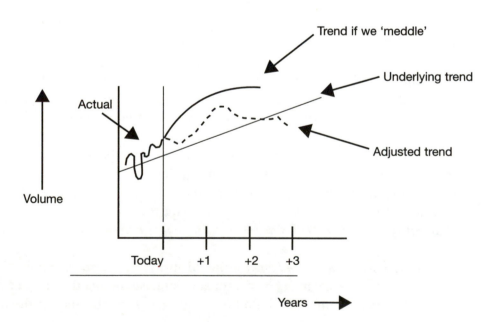

The only other adjustment to this figure that is necessary would be where you have decided, as part of your strategy, to influence the market growth (i.e. to undertake a market development strategy). In this instance you would need to adjust the size of the market to reflect the additional growth that you are assuming will result from implementation of your strategy – see Table 12 on page 76.

TABLE 11 FORECASTING IMPACT OF KEY TRENDS

PRODUCT:	Segment:						
DATA	Yr – 3	Yr – 2	Yr – 1	Current	Yr + 1	Yr + 2	Yr + 3
MARKET SEGMENT DATA							
Volume based on historical sales growth projection							
% growth							
Key trends							
Eradication therapy (–ve % growth)							
National formulary (+ve % growth)							
Competitor pricing strategy (+ve % growth)							
Development of improved H-Pylori testing (–ve % growth)							
Future volume based on key trends analysis							
% volume growth							

The product forecast

Implicit within any one strategy is an understanding of which opportunities you will focus on. Also, what the company will need to excel at to be competitive for these opportunities.

The next step is, therefore, to consider your *activity plan*. The purpose of these activities is to improve the competitive position of your product. Each activity will have an impact upon the future sales of your product. To evaluate this you need to define what you will be doing differently from last year.

The underlying trend forecast assumes that what you did last year will be continued. Therefore, a change in product performance must come from the difference between the two years' activities. It is the incremental effect that you will need to decide. Also, you will need to consider the scale and type of activity at a segment level. Thus, a product sales forecast needs to be completed for each target segment. For the balance of the market, forecast a market share based on your current competitive position.

TABLE 12   ADJUSTING MARKET GROWTH ACCORDING TO STRATEGY

PRODUCT:	Segment:						
DATA	Yr – 3	Yr – 2	Yr – 1	Current	Yr + 1	Yr + 2	Yr + 3
MARKET SEGMENT DATA							
Volume based on historical sales growth projection % growth							
Key trends Eradication therapy (–ve % growth) National formulary (+ve % growth) Competitor pricing strategy (+ve % growth) Development of improved H-Pylori testing (–ve % growth) Future volume based on key trends analysis % volume growth							
Volume based on Strategy % growth							

Note, the effect of your activities will be twofold:

1. There will be the immediate effect.
2. There will be the lasting effect.

Although it might be expected that all marketing activity will have both effects, this need not be the case. For example, in a fairly stable market it might be desirable to engage in an early discount sell-in to guarantee distribution and shut out the competition. The probability will be that this will yield an immediate benefit, but will also create a future negative effect, since we mortgaged future months' sales. On the other hand, a targeted campaign designed to switch competitor users to your product should create an immediate effect. Depending upon the competitive value of your product, it would be expected that you will retain some of these new customers permanently. This would represent a lasting effect over subsequent months.

Table 13 provides a framework for completing the product forecast for the target market segments. The section entitled a 'sanity checking the forecast' provides guidelines for forecasting your market share within the balance of the market.

The changes we can achieve will be dependent on the resources available, and therefore at least two strategies should be considered. Depending on the product and the situation these may be chosen from:

- *zero-based* current strategy, given future environment;
- *best case*, i.e. given unlimited resources, what would we do and how quickly?
- *most likely* – the most realistic investment strategy, bearing in mind the corporate priorities and the likely available resources.

Once the basis for a forecast has been arrived at, this must be open to discussion and amendment by the relevant executive teams who will have to fulfil the plans. The reasoning behind the forecast, therefore, must be spelled out so that there may be a

TABLE 13   FORECASTING THE PRODUCT SALES

	Yr – 3	Yr – 2	Yr – 1	Current	Yr + 1	Yr + 2	Yr + 3
PRODUCT SALES DATA							
Volume (units)							
Growth (absolute)							
% growth							
Value							
Average unit price							
Growth (absolute)							
% growth							
Net sales							
% growth							
MARKET SHARE DATA							
% Volume Market Share							
% Value Market Share							
Market Position (e.g. No 1, 2, etc.)							
Leading Competitor's Market Share %							

basis for *rational* disagreement. Once the forecast is agreed, there is an implication of managerial commitment to it.

Sanity checking the sales forecast

Our market share forecast will have considered:

- our competitive position;
- type of competitors;
- current competitor status:
  - how many prescriptions are written for major competitors?
  - are they gaining or losing share?
- their likely future strategy and how this affects our competitive position.

On the basis of this information we need to 'sanity check' how much of our future business is anticipated to come from market growth and how much from the competition.

The following examples will give broad guidance on how to use the SWOT decision to sanity check the forecast.

HIGH MARKET OPPORTUNITY – LOW COMPETITIVE STRENGTH

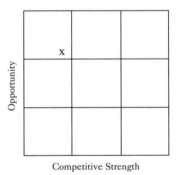

This will indicate that market growth will provide potential for increasing sales. However, the low competitive strength you possess will result in the bulk of this growth going to the competition. Therefore, you would expect a growth in your sales, but at a rate below that of the market, leading to a decline in market share.

Your forecast should reflect a year-on-year growth, but at a rate below that of the market. Any other position would not be congruent with your analysis.

HIGH MARKET OPPORTUNITY – HIGH COMPETITIVE STRENGTH

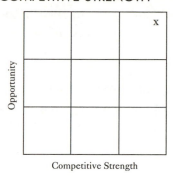

Again, this is a market which provides an opportunity for growth. However, you possess the greater strength to take advantage of this potential. As a result, you would expect to grow faster than the market and improve market share.

Your forecast should reflect a year-on-year growth, but at a rate that exceeds that of the market.

LOW MARKET OPPORTUNITY – HIGH COMPETITIVE STRENGTH

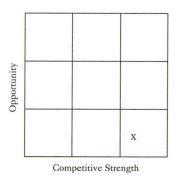

The market is presented as having little or no inherent growth potential, and you must look to taking sales from the competition to achieve growth. You are positioned as being stronger, so you will need to use this to seize sales. You should expect to increase market share but at a rate that is dependent upon the resistance presented by the 'habit' influence in the market.

Your forecast should reflect a year-on-year growth, at a rate greater than that of the market and be dependent upon the speed of conversion of competitive users.

LOW MARKET OPPORTUNITY – LOW COMPETITIVE STRENGTH

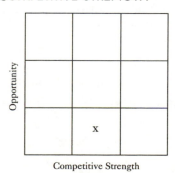

With no potential growth in the market and lacking competitive strength you will look to be at risk of losing sales and share to the competition. Your key concern will be to restrict this loss by reinforcing the habit influence, establishing defensive barriers and upgrading weakness areas.

Your forecast will reflect a year-on-year decline. The rate of this will depend upon the degree of resistance you can provide against the stronger competition, the degree of 'habit' influence in the market, and the speed at which you can correct your weaknesses.

The quarterly review

The key to justifiable forecasting is the conscientious adoption of a logical sequential marketing process. This enables cause and effect to be monitored. It provides a rationale for the forecast which can be evaluated in hindsight to provide experience-learning points. No one can say definitively that a certain action will produce a certain result. However, by comparing actual results with the forecast ones, it will be possible over time to become less inaccurate. This will only occur if the process of check analysis takes place, and this must cover under-, as well as over-performance. Experience comes from the recognition and correction of errors, not just from length of service.

THE APPROACH TO THE REVIEW

You should always review your actual performance against forecast and budget. It is particularly helpful in performing 'gap analysis', e.g. on current actions, it looks as if I will be 20 per cent below budget at the end of the year, and obviously to make budget I must increase my short-/medium-term marketing activity.

The forecasts are amended for internal consistency as the dialogue between the forecast expectation and the planning intention proceeds. This means that this type of forecast tends to be self-fulfilling.

Your sales forecast must reflect your marketing analysis. It is, therefore, essential that your analysis is as good as it can be. The sales forecast is an important self-evaluation tool. The ongoing comparison between the forecast and the actual is not just a figure: it should also be a thinking prompt.

Every gap between the two figures should lead to a consideration of the following checklist. Going through this series of questions and referring back to your marketing plan will help you to face the inevitable question of marketing – 'Your product is above/below budget. Why?'

Rather than the creative solution or the shoulder shrug, you will possess a rational answer. This may not get you completely off the hook, but at least it will be a 'professional' answer.

A CHECKLIST FOR THE REVIEW PROCESS:

1. Has the market responded as I thought?
   - If it has, the problem lies with the product performance.
   - If it has not, then the problem starts with the market analysis.
2. What has driven the market change?
   - Did I recognize the fact? – Data Supply Learning Point.
   - What effect did I expect?
   - What effect happened? – Analysis Learning Point.
3. Is the relationship between my product and the market as expected?
   - If it is, the forecasting error is exclusively with the market and environmental analysis and prediction.
   - If it is not, the cause lies in the company/product analysis and prediction.
4. From where did I expect to get sales?
   - Did I achieve this? – Analysis Learning Point.
   - What actions did I plan to happen?
   - Did they all happen as planned? – Control Management Learning Point.
   - Where did the action do better/worse than expected? – Experience Learning Point.

Expenditure forecasting

At the product/service level, return on investment can be more directly related to costs. In order to achieve each of the objectives in the marketing plan, a certain level of expenditure (investment) will be required. What will be the return for this expenditure? If we changed our objectives, could we achieve a higher return on our investment?

One of the aims in setting objectives in the marketing plan is to try to ensure that *the objectives chosen give the maximum possible return on investment*.

RETURN ON INVESTMENT

An extremely important concept in planning is that of 'return on investment'. It can apply at any level in the planning process. The interpretation and precise definition of the term will depend on the level at which it is used.

At whichever level it is used, return on investment is a way of measuring profitability. The important thing is that it measures profitability, *with reference to the investment associated with generating the income*. In the broadest sense, return on investment is a measure of income or profit divided by the investment required to help obtain the income or profit. It puts profit into context and helps to facilitate comparisons.

The level at which we are interested in exploring this concept is at the product/service and activity levels. However, ultimately, returns build up at each level and feed back into the one above. Among the long-term goals is to make the company profitable and to maximize the return for the owners (shareholders). This overall return on investment is the summation of returns for each product/service and activity level.

Because costs are relatively small in relation to returns, many people tend to focus on revenues rather than costs. However, as revenues are eroded – particularly through increasing regulation and competition – managers are looking at costs more and more.

To demonstrate how important it is to look at profits in relation to investment, look at this ranking of pharmaceutical companies in terms of turnover, profitability and return on investment.[1]

These graphs show how a different picture emerges, depending upon the measure of performance. While overall profit is important, return on investment is a key measure. It shows the opportunity cost to investors of investing their money in that particular company. The safest alternative would be to put their money in the bank at prevailing rates of interest.[2]

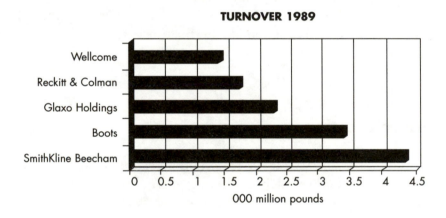

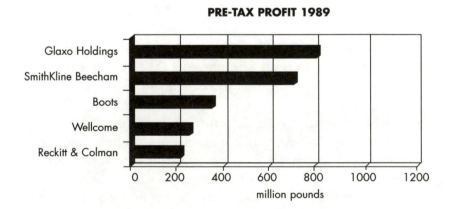

---

1 In this example 'return on investment' has been defined as pre-tax profit divided by net tangible assets. There are various ways of measuring 'investment': total assets; total assets employed; total assets less current liabilities; or stockholders' equity. 'Net tangible assets' are derived from the sum of revenue reserves, and provisions, capital reserves, ordinary issued share capital, other share capital, long-term loans, less intangibles.

2 However, it should be noted that 'return on investment' as defined here is not directly comparable with a return which could be earned from the bank.

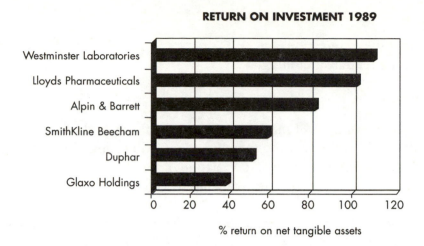

RETURN ON INVESTMENT 1989

% return on net tangible assets

It is important to think through each investment decision from your plan and try to assess what the extra resources will add. Can they be justified? In the case of advertising, mailings and discounting, it is difficult to forecast with any accuracy. However, it is important to think through what extra level of sales would be required in order to justify any additional expenditure. Every decision should be justified with reference to its return on investment.

It is also important to link expenditure back to objectives. Different situations will require different levels of investment: for instance, the investment required to hold sales compared with the investment required to defend a position and the investment required to hold a position.

Sales forecasting methods – an overview

Forecasting methods are mainly applied in forecasting sales and market demand. *Chambers* (1979) classified them in three categories:

1. Qualitative techniques.
2. Time series analysis.
3. Causal models.

In each category there is a series of models, some of which are suitable for forecasting initial sales and some for repeat sales. Consequently, it is important to use the technique most appropriate to the product and circumstances.

Probably the best known forecasting techniques are the *time series* methods. These rely on historical data, and so by definition are of limited application to the forecasting of new product sales. The exceptions are where the sales history of a similar product can give guidance, and where the product is only new to the company and not to the market.

Time series methods include:

1. trend extrapolations;
2. exponential smoothing.

TREND EXTRAPOLATIONS

A whole spectrum of methods exists with, at one end, the simple (probably very naive) 'sales will continue at the same level', or 'will change by a constant amount each year', and, at the other end, by extrapolation of time series curves using regression analysis to make the curve fit the data available.

Product managers are not expected to be expert in producing regression analyses, but it is worthwhile knowing why it is done and what the advantages and limitations are. The technique is based on developing a function which expresses the relationship between dependent and independent variables. It is used primarily in sales forecasting, but also for segmentation and consumer behaviour analysis, e.g. sales, and it can also provide measures of association between independent variables. It enables predictions about a dependent variable, e.g. sales, and it can also provide measures of association between independent variables, e.g. doctor time, and certain important marketing dependent variables, e.g. advertising space. The major limitation is that it requires finding the line of best fit, and in order to achieve this, all the important parameters have to be included (usually you will have to say what the important parameters are). It can become quite complex and therefore errors can creep in.

EXPONENTIAL SMOOTHING

This basically involves moving averages and weighting the more recent data more heavily. This method is based on the following model:

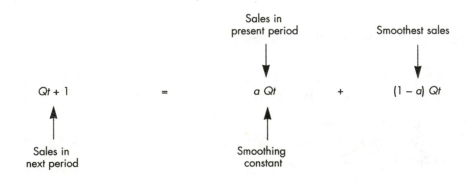

Where Qt is found by averaging the sales for the last few periods – in other words a moving average a is derived by trial-and-error testing of different constraints between 0 and 1, in order to find the one that gives the best fit of past sales.

In order to select a forecasting technique for new packs or sales, the first principle is to match the methodology with the situation. The degree of newness, product and market characteristics are all crucial, as are the forecaster's ability, urgency and the purpose for which the forecast is needed. Also critical are the range over which the forecast is operative and the comprehensibility and, therefore, acceptability to managers. Needless to say, there is no single forecasting method for all products. The second principle is that at least two methods should be used, and one of these should be the subjective judgment of the forecaster who should override the formal technique decision, if necessary. There are powerful arguments for combining forecasts by different techniques. Methods are selective in the information they use so that a combination of methods would incorporate more information and improve accuracy. *The important thing is that forecasts generated by machines are only as good as the information you put in, and your expertise is what makes the difference.*

PACK, VALUE, VOLUME?

One key question about the sales forecast is at what level should it be conducted. One school of thought is that all forecasts should be built up using pack-level forecasts, while another says that forecasts should be by value. In reality the level is to some extent determined by the product itself and the variety of packs and formulations which exists, and also what the forecast is being used for:

- Production forecasting needs to be done at pack level to ensure that the correct proportions of each pack is produced.
- Some products may have either very few packs, or one pack that is by far the biggest and it alone counts for most of the sales – here product level forecasting might be sufficient.
- Some products have a number of different formulations, and so it may be appropriate to forecast at formulation level.

Whatever the forecasting techniques used, it is important that the sales forecast is seen as part of the marketing planning process where, having identified what and to whom sales are going to be made, we quantify the value of the sales to be achieved and the revenue needed to achieve the sales.

7

Strategy Implementation

Introduction

As resources are limited, the extent to which you improve/maintain your competitive position is a management decision, and is invariably linked to the incremental return. Deciding what it is you need to invest in is an important process. By virtue of the way that we approach developing the plan, we are able to determine the priorities.

Selecting target segments within the context of strategy is the first step towards prioritizing where we are going to invest our limited resources. Within each target segment, we will be focusing on specific opportunities and threats, which in turn will help us decide which strengths and weaknesses are more important than others. These strengths and/or weaknesses are critical success factors (CSFs). Objectives will be set against each CSF so that it is very clear where we need to get to in relation to each CSF. These objectives then provide a mechanism through which we can prioritize activities.

In this chapter we provide guidelines for how we should go about identifying CSFs, setting objectives and defining the most appropriate tactics. Towards the end of the chapter we also discuss the considerations that you ought to give to message formulation and the role of the product manager as product champion.

Critical success factors

Critical success factors can be defined as

> The strengths that need to be maintained and/or exploited, and the weaknesses that need to be corrected in order to implement strategy successfully.

Not surprisingly, CSFs are derived from the strengths and weaknesses part of the SWOT analysis.

It is very easy to make long lists of critical success factors. However, what we need to do is to select the opportunities of which we wish to take advantage, and the threats that we need to manage. The *critical* success factors are the elements within our control that we should focus on to ensure we achieve the best result.

There is obviously no magic number, but based on best practice in other companies across various industries, it would seem that between five and seven CSFs are manageable: anything less than the minimum would result in narrow unchallenging plans; anything more would result in unfocused effort and a possible impact on the quality of execution.

Critical success factors can be chosen by using the following technique (based on Kotler) which judges strengths and weaknesses on a performance/importance scale, seen in Table 14 and Figure 15.

TABLE 14   STRENGTHS/WEAKNESSES ANALYSIS

SWOT	PERFORMANCE					IMPORTANCE		
Strength or weakness factor	Major strength	Minor strength	Neutral	Weak-ness	Major weak-ness	High	Med	Low
•								
•								
•								
•								
•								
•								
•								

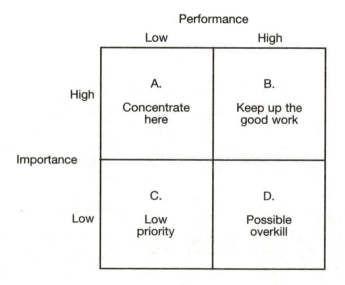

FIGURE 15   PERFORMANCE/IMPORTANCE MATRIX

Three points of importance for this technique are:

- critical success factors should be based on factors rating A & B;
- the critical success factor should be justified (i.e. the implication of not having it);
- input from anyone who contributed to the SWOT or who will be affected by the choice of the CSFs should be sought.

Setting marketing objectives

There is a tendency to focus on *financial* objectives when writing the marketing plan, because this is the 'bottom line' for most managers. As the plan gets relayed back up the hierarchy and, ultimately, to the board, text gets distilled, plans become summarized and numbers (particularly costs and revenues) are one of the few remaining features. Most people are aware that it is the numbers that will receive the widest scrutiny. Top management changes to the plan usually involve reducing expenditure or increasing revenue.

While this is the reality, the marketing plan is supposed to be a functioning document. Your marketing plan should tell you how you will achieve your sales targets. From the plan, you should be able to justify either an increase or a decrease in financial targets. You should be in a position to 'stick to your guns' in any subsequent review of expenditure process as a result of top management edicts.

Your working list of marketing objectives must, therefore, be more detailed and more specific. They are setting out what you need to achieve in order to meet the targets set out in Year 1 of the marketing plan. It might be helpful to make this distinction:

- The financial objectives set out in Year 1 of the strategic plan are *overall targets*.
- The marketing objectives are what are needed in order to meet these overall targets. They will be more detailed, not necessarily financial, and may even be segment-specific.

Against each Critical Success Factor, you need to set yourself an objective. These objectives relate to the five 'P's' involved in successful marketing:

- Product.
- Price.
- Promotion.
- Place.
- People.

Objectives need to be:

- Specific.
- Measurable.
- Ambitious.
- Realistic.
- Timed.

The tactical plan

Most of your *activities* should be linked to achieving your objectives (i.e. activities should be linked to the achievement of objectives rather than to CSFs). See Table 15.

Suppose the CSF is '100 per cent awareness of product with all physicians', and the related objective is 'hold current 100 per cent awareness levels with all physicians'. How will you do this? Through advertising? Through the sales force? Through mailings?

There is no scientific way of answering this question. People are paid to make judgments based on experience. Monitoring the results of activities in previous years and talking with other managers will obviously assist in this process.

TABLE 15   MARKETING ACTION PLAN TEMPLATE

This form provides a framework for developing the action plan.

PRODUCT:

ACTION PLAN																			
CSF: **Objective:**																			
Activity	Key	Code	Budget Actual	Start	End	Resp	Jan	Feb	Mar	April	May	June	July	Aug	Sept	Oct	Nov	Dec	Impact

The role of the product manager

Product managers need to behave like product champions:

- They are passionate about their product and/or project . . . they believe in it . . . they want it to succeed.
- They are self-motivating. They don't require promises of a reward or threats of punishment to ensure that they complete a project or manage a product.
- They have staying power. They see projects through from beginning to end, they don't give up at the first barrier.
- They have attention to detail, but will not lose sight of the vision for the product or project.
- They are innovative. Creativity is thinking up new things, but innovation is doing new things.
- They see weaknesses and threats as potential areas of strength and opportunity.
- They work well with other departments and external agencies. They recognize that they cannot achieve results on their own – they need the support of a team. They use the expertise and competence of others to complement their own areas of strength.
- They must be regarded as the experts on the product or project. They need to have up-to-date information (example, brand fact books) and be seen as the co-ordination reference point.
- They need to have a sense of ownership. They must feel responsible and accountable for the product or project (even when sometimes they are not).

'Product champions' have the know-how, energy, daring and staying power to implement ideas

Tom Peters *In search of excellence*[1]

WHY DO COMPANIES NEED PRODUCT CHAMPIONS?

Most companies operate on a vertical basis not a horizontal one. This means that the company is organized by individual function (for example, sales, marketing, manufacturing, etc.) not by process, activity or project (which involve the participation of many functions).

> *Example:* In a process such as a new product development, a manager in charge of formulation will ultimately report to their line manager in R & D, *not* to the manager in charge of the product.

Product champions are critical for the success of vertically-organized companies, because they provide a means of operating horizontally on a product/project basis. The product champion will get things done across the company *without* real authority. Working horizontally means that the right activities are done at the right time by the right people.

The ability to operate horizontally will depend on the strength of the product champion. Companies need product champions to ensure that projects are carried through from

---

1 T.J. Peters and R. Waterman (1984) *In search of excellence: lessons from America's best-run companies* (paperback), Harper & Row.

start to finish. One person is needed to focus on the project, so that the issues and priorities by functions do not distract management.

Product champions are the custodians of brands. They must guard against decisions which could harm the intrinsic value of the brand (e.g. manufacturing cost savings which will improve the profitability, but could harm the brand's effectiveness).

8

Communications and its Role in Strategy Implementation

Communication in one form or another is likely to emerge as a critical success factor. Thus, the communications plan is an integral part of executing the marketing strategy.

A significant 'marketing' development is the move towards integrating marketing communications. Each marketing mix element is multidimensional, and includes a number of decision areas. Each must consider and contribute to the overall communications strategy. Thus, we need to examine how the *Product*, the *Price* and *Distribution* channels influence and interact with *Promotion*.

Today, the value of doing this is understood: companies can avoid duplication, take advantage of synergy among various communication tools, and develop more efficient and effective marketing communications programmes.

Within promotion today we are seeing a shift in expenditure from media advertising to other forms of promotion. Many marketeers feel that traditional media advertising has become too expensive and is therefore no longer cost-effective. Also, escalating price competition has resulted in marketeers pouring more of their promotional budgets into price promotions than into media advertising. Generally, there is increasing recognition that one should not be tied to the traditional mix, but rather should use whatever contact methods offer the best way of delivering the message to the target audience(s).

In conclusion, decisions need to be made with regard to the most effective communications style, media, and tools, to deliver the communication objectives to the target audience. Accurately broadcasting the right message to the correct constituency at the right time is critical to the success of any product, however large or small it is.

Thus, there is a need to understand how to manage each element of the promotional mix to achieve an effective communications strategy, and how to consider the other elements within the marketing mix in order to develop such a strategy. There is also a need to learn how to develop advertising objectives and strategies, a creative strategy, a media strategy, how to measure and test buyer response to marketing communications, and how to manage the relationship between the client and the agency. Finally, there is a need to understand current practices in advertising, sales promotion, public relations, and direct marketing and personal selling. This section addresses these issues.

The promotional mix

Each element of the promotional mix plays a distinctive role in a communications programme. Below is a summary of the role that each might play, the form that they might take, and their advantages.

A successful communications strategy requires that one finds the right combination of promotional tools and techniques, defines their role and the extent to which they can or should be used, and co-ordinates their use. To accomplish this, the marketer must understand the role of promotion in the marketing programme.

While implicit communication occurs through the various elements of the marketing mix, most of one's communications with the marketplace take place in a planned and controlled *promotional programme* (often referred to as the promotional campaign). The basic tools used to accomplish this programme are often referred to as the *promotional mix* (see Table 16).

Deciding on the creative strategy

The purpose of the promotions mix is to carry a message to the target segment in order to produce a desired response or attitude.

Before messages (i.e. the creative strategy) can be formulated, an in-depth understanding of the target segment is necessary:

- What is the profile of the segment?
- What are the key attitudes?
- How do the customers in each segment perceive the product and its competitors?
- What stage is the segment in the buying decision process?
- What desired response do we want to elicit?

SEGMENTATION IS ONLY MEANINGFUL IF IT IS USED AS A TOOL FOR UNDERSTANDING THE CUSTOMER SO THAT WE CAN INFLUENCE THEIR BEHAVIOUR I.E. TO BUY MORE OF OUR PRODUCTS.

THE WAY IN WHICH BEHAVIOUR CAN BE CHANGED IS THROUGH SENDING *MESSAGES* VIA THE *COMMUNICATIONS MIX*.

THE CUSTOMERS' DECISION-MAKING PROCESS

The purpose of any promotion must be to change attitudes of the target audience. The belief is that a change in attitude will result in a change in behaviour. Figure 16 provides

TABLE 16 PROMOTIONAL MIX OPTIONS

PROMOTIONAL MIX ELEMENT	ROLE	FORM	ADVANTAGES
Advertising	Non-personal communication about the company, a product, a service or an idea	Involves mass media (e.g. TV, radio, magazines, newspapers, Internet)	• Cost-effective when communicating with large audiences • Successful at creating the image/ symbolic appeal which is particularly important when it is difficult to differentiate the product/service on the basis of its functional attributes
Direct Marketing	Direct communication with target customers to generate a response and/or a transaction	It involves a variety of activities, including: database management, direct selling, telemarketing, direct response advertising.	• Convenience of shopping by mail or phone • Capability to target, and therefore cost-effective • Effective across all stages of the buying process
Sales Promotion	Those activities that provide extra value or incentives to the sales force, distributors, or even the ultimate customers and can stimulate immediate sales. Typically considered under two categories: • Customer/ consumer oriented sales promotion • Trade-oriented sales promotion	1. *Customer-oriented sales promotion.* This includes: sampling, rebates, contests, and various point of purchase materials. These tools encourage the customer to make an immediate purchase and thus can stimulate short-term sales. 2. *Trade-oriented sales promotion.* This type of promotion is targeted at the 'intermediaries', e.g. wholesalers, distributors and retailers/pharmacists. It is used to encourage the trade to stock and promote a company's products.	• There is increased consumer sensitivity to promotional deals, particularly when all else is perceived as being equal • Cost-effective
Publicity/Public Relations	The systematic planning for, and distribution of, information in an attempt to control and manage the image of the company/ product, and the nature of the publicity it receives is the function of public relations.	Public relations uses publicity and a variety of other tools, including special publications, sponsorship of special events/equipment, and participating in local/ community activities to enhance the organization's image. Advertising can also be used as a public relations tool.	• Breadth of coverage • Can be a powerful way of affecting awareness, knowledge, opinions and/ or behaviour because of its perceived independence • Perceived as more credible than a lot of other forms of communication • Low cost, i.e. costs incurred are largely costs in developing publicity items. The company is not typically paying for time or space in mass media communication channels

TABLE 16 CONCLUDED

PROMOTIONAL MIX ELEMENT	ROLE	FORM	ADVANTAGES
Publicity/ Public Relations continued	Publicity, on the other hand, refers to the non-personal communication regarding a company, a product, a service or an idea which is not directly paid for.		
Personal Selling	This person-to-person communication attempts to assist/ persuade prospective customers to purchase/use the company's product or service, or to act on an idea.	This involves person-to person communication which can take place face-to-face, at exhibitions, at meetings, or over the telephone and, today, also using the Internet.	● Immediate and precise feedback ● Ability to modify/tailor message according to the situation ● Ability to target
Interactive Marketing	Interactive marketing is a continously expanding discipline in which new tools are frequently being developed.	Interactive marketing can involve vehicles like the World Wide Web, Usenets, Electronic Mail, Mailing Lists, CD-ROMs, Fax-on-Demand, Multimedia Kiosks. (See Glossary of Marketing Terms.)	● A form of communication that is receiving a lot of attention. ● Can be relatively inexpensive. ● Access/coverage ● Targeting capability

a framework for considering the customer's decision-making process and the resulting communication challenges.

FORMULATING THE MESSAGE

Formulating the message requires solving four problems:

What to say	⇨	message content
how to say it (logically)	⇨	message structure
how to say it (symbolically)	⇨	message format
who should say it	⇨	message source

WHAT TO SAY – MESSAGE CONTENT

The product manager must decide what to say to the target segment to produce the

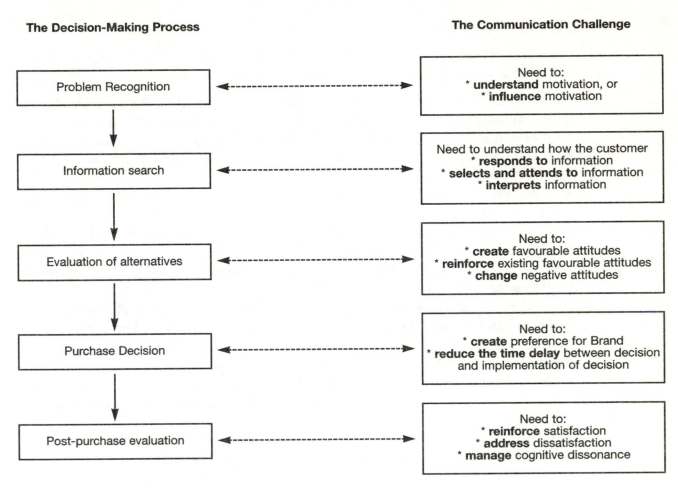

FIGURE 16 THE DECISION-MAKING PROCESS

desired response or the change in behaviour. Central to the content of the message is the unique selling proposition (the USP) – i.e. the benefit/motivation or reason why the customer should think about, evaluate and/or hopefully buy your product. There are basically three types of proposition:

1. *Rational proposition* – this proposition appeals to a customer's self-interest. It shows the product will deliver the claimed benefits. Examples would be messages demonstrating the product's performance, quality or economy. This type of appeal works well in the pharmaceutical industry where the customer gathers information in order to evaluate the alternatives.

2. *Emotional proposition* – this proposition attempts to arouse negative or positive emotions that will motivate a purchase. Examples of negative emotions used in advertising are fear, guilt and shame, while positive emotions are love, pride, joy and humour.

3. *Moral proposition* – the proposition is directed at the customer's sense of what is right and proper. They are often social causes and charities. Moral propositions are most effective when they are *moderately discrepant* with what the customer believes – messages that state only what the customer believes attract less attention and, at best, only reinforce beliefs, whereas messages that are too discrepant with the customer's beliefs will be counterargued in the customer's mind and then rejected.

HOW TO SAY IT LOGICALLY – MESSAGE STRUCTURE

A message's effectiveness depends on its structure as well as its content. Extensive research has been carried out on the relative effectiveness of three types of structure:

1. *Conclusion drawing* – this structure raises the question whether the manager should draw a definite conclusion for the customer, or let the customer draw the conclusion for themselves. It is generally thought that it is best to allow customers to reach their own decision, as conclusion-drawing causes negative reactions particularly in the following situations:
   - If the communicator is untrustworthy, the customer might resent the attempt to influence them.
   - If the issue is simple or the audience is intelligent (example physicians), they might be annoyed at the attempt to explain the obvious.
   - If the issue is highly personal, the audience might resent the communicator's attempt to draw a conclusion for them.

2. *One- or two-sided arguments* – this structure raises the question of whether the communicator should only praise the product or also mention some of its shortcomings. It may seem obvious that only one-sided presentations would be the most effective, but this structure does have its limitations:
   - One-sided messages work best with audiences that are initially predisposed to the product's position – two-sided arguments work better with audiences who are opposed.
   - Two-sided arguments work better with more intelligent audiences (note physicians).
   - Two-sided arguments are more effective with audiences who are likely to be exposed to counter-propaganda.

3. *Order of presentation* – this structure raises the question whether the communicator should raise the strongest argument first or last. In the case of the one-sided argument presenting the strongest message first has the advantage of establishing attention and interest. In the two-sided argument it is better to present the strongest argument last if the audience is opposed to the product, i.e. start with the other side's argument to disarm the customer and then conclude with your own strong argument.

HOW TO SAY IT SYMBOLICALLY – MESSAGE VISUALIZATION

The 'visualization' of the message will depend upon the medium used to convey the message.

Example:

- In a print ad the headline, illustration and copy will be important elements of the 'visualization' of the message.
- In one-to-one selling, the sales representative's knowledge, dress, manner and timeliness will be important.
- If the message is conveyed in the packaging, the size, language, colour, smell, etc. will be important.

WHO SHOULD SAY IT – MESSAGE SOURCE

Messages delivered by attractive sources achieve higher attention and recall. This refers to consumer goods such as Pepsi or Lucozade or, in the pharmaceuticals industry, using opinion leaders to convey the message implicitly that the product is the best for the treatment of a particular disease or condition.

The factors which underline source credibility are:

- *expertise* – the specialized knowledge that the source appears to possess to back the charm;
- *trustworthiness* – how objective and honest the source is perceived to be;
- *likeability* – how attractive the source is to the audience.

OTHER CONSIDERATIONS

1. Messages that have a single benefit/appeal are more effective than those with multiple benefits/appeals. This is particularly important to remember for mailings.
2. Messages communicated to a specific segment during a given time period should be consistent across the different elements of the communications mix.
3. Research carried out found that messages which are:
   - desirable (i.e. which say something desirable or interesting about the product),
   - exclusive (i.e. which say something that is distinctive),
   - believeable (i.e. the claim is believed or can be proved),

   are the most effective at changing customers' behaviour.

The key messages listed in marketing plans should have a rationale explaining why they have been selected and how they will change the behaviour of the majority of the customers in the segment.

GUIDELINES FOR EVALUATING CREATIVE OUTPUT

- Is the creative approach consistent with the brand's marketing and advertising objectives?
- Is the creative approach consistent with the creative strategy and objectives? Does it communicate what it is supposed to?
- Is the creative approach appropriate for the target audience?
- Does the creative approach communicate a clear and convincing message to the customer?
- Does the creative execution keep from overwhelming the message?
- Is the creative approach appropriate for the media environment in which it is likely to be seen?
- Is the concept truthful and tasteful?

The communications process

The ingredients of an effective promotional strategy include:
- identifying the target audiences;
- selecting the promotional mix elements, balancing the strengths and weaknesses of each;
- developing the messages to be conveyed;

- deciding how to combine the different promotional mix elements to achieve the marketing and promotional objectives;
- planning distribution strategies;
- designing evaluation methods.

In the development of a communications strategy, there is a need to refer back to the *situational analysis* in the Marketing Plan.

1. *The external analysis* focused on understanding the marketplace. An important part of the external analysis is the detailed consideration given to the customer's characteristics and buying patterns, their decision processes and the factors influencing their purchase decisions. The response process for products or services where the customer's decision-making is characterized by a high level of interest is often different from that for low-involvement or routine purchase decisions. These differences will influence the promotional strategy. The external analysis also considered factors such as the competitors. Your understanding of their segmentation, targeting and positioning, and promotion strategies is critical to designing an effective communications programme. Consideration also needs to be given to the size and allocation of their promotional budgets, their media strategies and the messages that they are sending to the marketplace.

2. *The internal analysis* assessed relevant areas involving the product/service offering and the capabilities of the company itself – specifically, the capabilities of the company/or the team to develop and implement a successful communications programme. For example, if this analysis highlighted the fact that the company is not capable of planning, implementing and managing certain areas of the communications programme, then it will be wise to identify an external agency that offers these capabilities.

SETTING COMMUNICATIONS OBJECTIVES

These are often stated in terms of the nature of the message to be communicated, or what specific communication effects are to be achieved. Communications objectives may include: creating awareness about a product and its attributes or benefits; developing favourable attitudes; or preference or even purchase intention. They serve as the guiding force for the overall communications strategy and of the objectives for each promotional mix element.

DETERMINING THE BUDGET

Your attention should turn to the promotional budget. Two basic questions need to be answered. What will the communications programme cost? How will this money be allocated? In an ideal world, the spend on promotion is driven by what *must* be done to accomplish the communication objectives. In reality, budgets are often determined by using a simplistic approach, such as: how much money is available? Or simply as a percentage of the brand's sales revenue. At this stage the budget is tentative. It can only be finalized once the communication strategies have been developed and approved.

DEVELOPING THE COMMUNICATIONS PROGRAMME

At this stage there is a need to decide the role and importance of each element of the promotions mix, and their co-ordination with one another. Each element of the mix should have its own set of objectives and a budget and strategy for meeting them.

Two important elements of the advertising strategy are *creative strategy* and *media strategy*.

1. The *creative strategy* involves determining the basic appeal and the message to the target audience. This process, along with the concepts that result, is to many the most fascinating aspect of promotion.
2. The *media strategy* involves determining which communications channels will be used to deliver the message to the target audience.

ESTABLISHING PROCESSES FOR MONITORING AND CONTROL

It is essential that there are processes in place to determine how well the communications plan is meeting the communications objectives. Not only do you want to know how well it is doing, but why. For example, if there were a problem, it might lie in the nature of the message or the communication channel used. You must understand the reason for the results in order to take corrective action.

Integrating the other elements in the marketing mix with promotion

Implicit communication occurs through the various elements of the marketing mix, and the marketing process involves combining the various elements of the marketing mix into a cohesive, effective, marketing programme. Therefore, each marketing mix element must consider and contribute to the overall communications strategy. Now we examine how the product, the price and distribution channels influence and interact with promotion.

THE PRODUCT

A product is not just a physical object, but a bundle of benefits or values that satisfies the needs of the customers and consumers. The needs may be purely functional, or may include social and psychological benefits. The term *product symbolism* refers to what a product (brand) means to consumers, and what they experience in purchasing and using it. Thus, when the product is being considered, it involves decisions not only about the item itself but also aspects such as service and guarantees, as well as the brand name and package design. In an effective communications programme the promotion, branding and packaging are all designed to present an image or positioning of the product that extends well beyond its 'function' attributes.

- *Branding:* choosing a brand name for a product is important from a promotional perspective because brand names communicate attributes and meaning. The brand name should help position the product in the customers' mind.
- *Brand equity:* this can be thought of as an intangible asset of added value or goodwill that results from the favourable image, impressions of differentiation, and/or strength

of customer/consumer attachment to a company name, brand name or trade mark. Brand equity allows a brand to earn higher volume sales or higher margins than it could without the name, thereby providing the company with competitive advantage.

- *Packaging:* traditionally, the package provided functional benefits such as economy, protection and storage. Today, however, many companies view the package as an extremely important vehicle for communicating with the consumer. Many products use packaging to create a distinct brand image and identity. It can also make the product more convenient to use and can convey important information.

THE PRICE

From a marketing communications perspective, the price must be consistent with the perceptions about the product, as well as the communications strategy. A product positioned as highest quality but carrying a lower price will only confuse the customers. In other words, the price must support the product's positioning.

Several interesting discoveries concerning the interaction of promotion, price and product quality emerged from the Profit Impact of Marketing Strategies (PIMS) project of the Strategic Planning Institute. These included the fact that:

- brands with relatively high promotion budgets were able to charge premium prices;
- companies with high-quality products charge high relative prices for the extra quality, but businesses with high-quality and high-promotion levels obtained the highest prices;
- companies with high prices and high promotion-expenditure levels showed a greater return on investment than those with relatively low prices and low promotion-expenditure levels;
- companies with high-quality products suffered the most, in terms of return on investment, when the promotion and pricing strategies were inconsistent with the 'quality' of product on offer.

DISTRIBUTION

An important decision involves the way one makes the products and/or services available for purchase. A quality product is of little value unless it is available *where* the consumer wants it, *when* they want it and *with the proper support and service*.

There are examples of how the distribution channel can contribute to communications. For example, a premium-priced product like Eprex (EPO) is distributed direct to the retail chemist in order that the retailer does not have to tie up money in stock (reinforces the premium price), and to ensure that the company retains control over the way in which the product is distributed (reinforcing the 'quality' image of the product).

Whether to emphasize a push or pull strategy for a product depends on a number of factors:

- Its relationship with the trade.
- Its promotional budget.
- The likely demand for the product.

Where you need to encourage the wholesaler/distributor to stock and promote the product, a push strategy is typically used, whereas, when the demand outlook is favourable because the product has unique benefits, a pull strategy may be appropriate.

The role of the external agency

The main reason for using outside agencies is that they provide the client with the services of highly-skilled individuals who are specialists in their chosen fields. The agency will draw on the broad range of experience it has gained while working on a diverse set of marketing problems for various clients. There are many different types of agency, performing different services and, consequently, organized differently.

Full service agencies are ones which offer their clients a full range of marketing, communications and promotions services. Typically, this includes planning, creating, producing, performing research, and selecting media. At the other extreme we find *specialist agencies*. These specialize in a particular type of business and use their knowledge of this area to assist clients. Irrespective of the type of agency involved, the following typical functions will be present in some form or other:

- The account management team will be responsible for the link between the 'creative team' and the 'client'. Depending on the size of the client and its budget, there may be one or more account executives assigned to the account team. The account manager is responsible for understanding the client's needs and interpreting them to the creative team. They are also responsible for co-ordinating efforts in the planning, creation and production of the promotional materials, presenting the agency's recommendations to the client and obtaining client approval.
- Many of the full service agencies will retain a research department. Their function is to gather, analyse and interpret information that will be useful in developing and executing the communications strategy.
- The creative department is responsible for the creation and execution of advertisements. Copywriters conceive the ideas for the ads, and write the headlines, subheads and body copy. While copywriters are responsible for what the message says, the art department is responsible for developing concepts that will communicate the key points which have been determined to be the basis of the creative strategy. The writers and artists generally work under the direction of the agency's creative director.
- The production department is responsible for producing the finished items. Typically, they receive copy, layout, illustrations and mechanical specifications from the creative team and are required to produce the final item to a deadline and within a budget.

THE ADVERTISING AGENCY BRIEF

'Rubbish in, rubbish out' is an old expression. Briefing an advertising agency conjures up different thoughts in different people.

Marketing personnel who are experienced in this field themselves often disagree on some of the details of briefing agencies, but the fundamental points are as follows:

- Briefing an agency is an exercise in motivation and communication – treat it as such;
- You will expect a professional execution of concepts from your agency – they should expect no less of your briefing;
- They will not tell you how to market your product, so do not tell them how to advertise – but do make sure they understand your sales techniques;
- Do tell them what you want the promotion to do, not what it ought to be.

The steps in briefing should be:

1. briefing of product/service and therapy area;
2. trends in the marketplace that are important, including competition;
3. relevant opportunities, threats, strengths and weaknesses;
4. your strategy, and the positioning you want for your product/service;
5. your tactical objectives;
6. timing;
7. budget;
8. documentary evidence and written briefs.

WHAT HAPPENS TO THE BRIEF?

The first step in the creative process should be the evolution of a creative strategy. The account executive and/or account manager will convert your brief into so called 'agency speak'. This should answer the following questions:

To whom are we talking?

In other words how are we defining the target audience and what are the alternatives?

What do we want them to do?

What are the goals of the advertising or promotion in terms of action we are expecting the target audience to take (e.g. continue prescribing at the same level)?

What do they have to think and feel if they are to do it?

In order to answer this we clearly need to know what they think and feel now, and how realistic change is within a given time-frame.

What do we have which will help them think and feel this way?

The answer may involve new information on the product, or more money or more time, and so on.

What else?

In this section any information likely to be relevant but not covered elsewhere will be included. Examples might be: quality of sales force; the introduction of new competitors, etc. You should ask to see a copy of the internal creative brief!

EVALUATING AGENCIES

Given the significant amounts of money spent on communication, regular reviews of the agency's performance is necessary. The evaluation process should involve two types of assessment: a) the *financial audit* (this focuses on how the agency conducts its own business), and b) the *qualitative audit* (this focuses on the agency's efforts in the planning, developing and implementing of the communications programmes and considers the results achieved).

The review process provides both parties (i.e. client and agency) with an understanding of the potential problems, enabling them to take corrective action and therefore avoid them.

An example of an agency-evaluation system is shown in Figure 17 (pages 106–8).

Communications agencies' perspectives of the pharmaceutical industry

HOW DO THEY TYPICALLY DESCRIBE THE TYPE OF WORK THAT THEY UNDERTAKE?

There was a different response from advertising agencies from that received from PR agencies.

ADVERTISING AGENCIES

Although a lot of agencies specialize in healthcare, because they work with a wide range of products across a number of areas (e.g. OTC, pharmaceuticals, medical equipment, etc.), they do not consider themselves 'specialists'.

The activities undertaken by agencies vary enormously. They range from *strategy*, through *planning* and *communication* to *advertising*, *promotion* and *branding*. Generally speaking, clients use them to put together a promotional campaign, which usually means a press ad, a sales aid, direct mail and congress support.

As companies increasingly recognize the influence of audiences other than the prescriber, this is affecting the promotion effort, i.e. the campaign is becoming broader and deeper.

PR AGENCIES

PR is about communicating change, whether that change is taking place internally or externally. PR activities, therefore, range from preparing organizations for communicating change, supporting the communication process, through to evaluating the impact of the changes occurring. PR should not be used alone.

Typically PR agencies work with different industries and specialize in one aspect of PR. The agency we spoke to specializes in issues/crisis management.

Please score each set of criteria between 1 and 5, where 1 = poor, 2 = satisfactory, 3 = good, 4 = very good, 5 = excellent. At the end of each session please comment on your assessment.

1.   Strategic Ability

	1	2	3	4	5
Understanding of brief					
Interpretation					
Grasp of objectives					
Analytical skills					
Judgment					

Comments

....

....

....

2.   Planning Ability

	1	2	3	4	5
Grasp of logistics					
Prioritisation					
Relation to business objectives					
Budgeting					

Comments

....

....

....

FIGURE 17   AGENCY EVALUATION CRITERIA

3. Quality of Programme

	1	2	3	4	5

Relevance

Innovation/originality

Workable ideas

Resource allocation (people/time)

Comments

....

....

....

4. Team Dynamics

	1	2	3	4	5

Client interaction

Team interaction

Team role clarity

Enthusiasm

Staff turnover

Key account handlers

Comments

....

....

....

FIGURE 17 CONTINUED

5.   Team Skill Base

1	2	3	4	5

CVs/relevant experience/expertise

Writing ability

Media contacts

Creative ability

Comments

....

....

....

6.   Financial Management

1	2	3	4	5

Costs incurred explicit

Invoices received promptly

Resource allocation (people/time)

Comments

....

....

....

Figure 17   Concluded

They will usually be involved in preparing the market for a new product launch, supporting the process of building awareness, and dealing with medical issues and their impact on the commercial continuity of a particular product or therapeutic area.

IS THERE A GAP BETWEEN WHAT AGENCIES HAVE TO OFFER AND WHAT THE INDUSTRY USES THEM FOR?

Yes – typically the *advertising agency* feels it is treated as a design house. This has two significant implications:

1. Agencies feel that their involvement in the development of communication strategy can be limited. They feel they should be seen as the communication experts.
2. Agencies feel that generally there is a poor understanding of developing brand identity/brand essence. This is definitely perceived to be an area where the industry is missing out on the agencies' expertise.

The answer from the *PR agency* was also 'yes'. They too feel they are used 'tactically', i.e. when the issue has turned into a crisis. Generally speaking, they would argue most organizations are ill-prepared in terms of business and communication processes when it comes to anticipating the impact of certain issues and having a plan in place to deal with the most significant ones.

ARE THE CONSTRAINTS YOU HAVE TO RESPECT WHEN WORKING WITH THE INDUSTRY REAL OR PERCEIVED?

REAL

When working with the pharmaceutical industry there is obviously the 'code of practice' which leaves room for interpretation. The Company Medical Director is the ultimate decision-maker in this area. This does pose some problems:

- Very often the medical director is not involved enough in the process to understand what the agency is trying to do with the communications strategy.
- Interpretation of the code will always be subjective.
- Often there is a time-lag between the submission of a concept by the agency and the Medical Director's approval/rejection thereof. If it is rejected, this can often leave the agency with as little as 24 hours to come up with a new concept.
- Medical Directors generally 'mistrust' communications agencies.

While a Code of Practice is real, it does not constitute a barrier to creativity. The best creative work in the 'healthcare arena' proves that it is an opportunity, not a problem, and should not be treated as such.

PERCEIVED

- Timing can be a real source of frustration. Agencies are often expected to assimilate all the background information and come up with a successful communications strategy in a very short period of time.
- Asking the agency to develop a communication campaign for a product which already

has a name, a logo, packaging, etc. All these aspects contribute to brand identity and influence the communication strategy.

HOW WOULD YOU DESCRIBE THE ROLE OF THE AGENCY IN THE CLIENT/AGENCY RELATIONSHIP?

The primary role of all agencies is to meet the client's specific needs. They do, however, also see themselves as having an important role in:

- helping the product manager make the right decision;
- training and developing the product manager, who is usually young and inexperienced;
- maintaining continuity of the brand (typically a new product manager wants to make changes). Where there has been a long-established relationship with the client, the agency is often best placed to do this;
- influencing the long-term thinking behind the 'branding' process. The agency is often better equipped to do this than the product manager;
- supporting tactical implementation – for example, media relations, event management, symposia organization, resource packs, and communication programmes.

HOW WOULD YOU DESCRIBE THE CLIENT'S ROLE?

The client should:
- understand the commonality of the goals between the agency and themselves;
- define and set the objectives;
- be able to differentiate their marketing USP from the message that they want to communicate;
- praise when credit is due;
- trust the agency;
- be strong project managers. Nowadays there is a wider variety of people from different agencies working together. This requires strong project management and co-ordination skills.

The clients who get the best out of the agency are usually ones who are:

- rigorous;
- challenging;
- demanding;
- yet, open-minded.

HOW IN YOUR OPINION COULD COMMUNICATION BETWEEN THE AGENCY AND THE CLIENT BE IMPROVED?

In most situations there is a lack of contact at the senior level.

The general view is that the development of the communication strategy should be a team-based effort with more senior people involved at the critical stages of the process. This is particularly important in the light of the lack of training and experience of the young marketeer. Often a lot of responsibility is delegated to the product manager.

It is generally believed that the communication process would improve if the product manager had more formal training.

HOW DO YOU EVALUATE YOUR SUCCESS?

There are:

- *quantitative parameters*: for example – awareness, usage, levels of recommendation, media response, level of impact of crisis;
- *qualitative and subjective parameters*: for example – the process, the data.

In practice, clients are not necessarily willing to share the data with you, or willing to invest in further research to evaluate performance. However, there is growing acceptance that it is important to evaluate performance. It is important that, if evaluation is carried out, the right questions are asked. So, communication with the market research agency who will be doing the research is critical.

WHAT ELEMENTS DO YOU NEED TO HAVE IN PLACE TO OPTIMIZE YOUR CHANCES OF ACHIEVING SUCCESS?

- A *core team in place* (marketeer, senior manager, market research manager and account manager).
- A *good brief* (one that provides a clear idea of what is wanted from the agency, provides as much background information as possible, sets out clear objectives, explains how the results will be measured and how they will evaluate the proposal, and gives the agency a reasonable amount of time).
- A *good relationship*. Trust, professional respect, confidence and willingness to give positive feedback are all important aspects of developing this relationship.
- *Project management*. There is a need to spend time on goal definition so that everyone 'buys in' to the goals. If any doubt emerges about the agency work, this should be raised as soon as possible. Any changes that need to be made should be made by the agency – to do this they need only understand where and why. The product manager needs to be convinced about the communication strategy so that they can defend it if appropriate, and accept good suggestions where appropriate.
- *The right attitude*. Avoid arrogance and complacency. Create smarter/more innovative ways of using communication expertise.

CREATIVE WORK CHECKLIST

Creative work follows on from the creative strategy. It involves a leap, but certain criteria may usefully be employed when evaluating creative material. These include:

- *relevance:* a creative idea, however exciting, is of little value if it is 'off strategy'. It must be relevant or it is 'pure art';
- *originality:* since the object of creative material such as advertising matter is to stimulate a response from the audience, it must not only be relevant but also original. One without the other is not cost-effective advertising;
- *simplicity:* generally speaking, effective communication gets across one idea. As a result the respondent can say about the product 'it's the one that . . .'. Simplicity is the key to success;
- *property:* too much advertising is generic. You can substitute the name of a competitor at the bottom without anyone noticing. Creative advertising should involve a visual or

verbal property unique to the brand (e.g. 'The beer that gets to the parts other beers can't reach'). This contributes significantly to building brands;

- *impact/interest:* advertising that seeks to make an impact purely for the sake of it is likely to be counter-productive. Advertising should be interesting rather than strident;
- *tone of voice:* the way in which a message is delivered is as important as the message itself. It is therefore vital to consider whether the tone of voice is right (i.e. too flippant, too austere);
- *interpretation:* it is important to remember that advertising can always convey the unintended, sometimes with disastrous results. It pays to check this out. Research has a role in evaluating advertising, but because of its artificiality and, often, naivety it should always be regarded as merely as an aid to judgment.

9

Marketing Research

The product manager becomes of most value to himself and his company when he realizes that he is an important 'interface' in the company, who has to be the product 'expert', able to communicate recommendations as to future actions and act upon decisions that affect the product. Research will play an important role, helping managers make better, more informed decisions. Marketing decision-makers rely on information supplied by marketing research to support the decision-making process, because it is believed that this reduces the level of risk in making a 'wrong' decision.

For many companies in healthcare-related industries a well-staffed internal marketing research department is a luxury that cannot be supported in an era of tight cost controls and corporate downsizing. As a result, product or department managers with little formal training in the research discipline are forced to outsource critical marketing studies.

Furthermore, marketing research is rarely cheap or easy to obtain and, in fact, may constitute a significant investment in itself. It is essential, therefore, that it is used to support 'critical' decisions and that the information that is obtained is *timely, useful and accurate*.

These are just some of the reasons why an appreciation of marketing research is necessary.

The marketing research process

There are many components in the marketing research process, from basic problem definition to determining what kind of information you need to be gathered, how it should be gathered, and how it should be analysed.

The basic steps in any research operation are:

1. formulating the research problem;
2. determining the research design;
3. determining the data collection method;
4. designing the data collection form;
5. designing the sample and collecting the data;

6. analysing and interpreting the data;
7. preparing the research report.

The kind of information that you need to gather might be *quantitative* or *qualitative*.

- *Qualitative research* refers to research that cannot be analysed statistically. The primary use of this type of research is in the early stages of research to find, explore, develop and discover such things as: needs or opportunities; new product concepts; product positioning; advertising and communication concepts; questionnaires; attitude and behavioural effects. Generally it uses in-depth interviews, group discussions or focus groups.
- *Quantitative research* refers to research which endeavours to produce data in hard numbers. For example 10 per cent of doctors prescribe product *x* at least twice a week. Generally it uses structured questionnaires and is a large undertaking.

Information can be collected either through reading (referred to as desk research or secondary research), or through contacting people (referred to as primary research). When contacting people, there are a number of research options. These include:

- focus groups (in person, telephone, Internet);
- in-depth personal interview;
- telephone surveys;
- intercepts (at events);
- mail surveys;
- internet surveys;
- telephone discussion groups;
- test market services.

Outlined in Figure 18 is a simple flow diagram, highlighting the key issues to be considered when deciding what kind of research should be undertaken. We will then go on to discuss the different types of research in more detail.

Types of research

SECONDARY RESEARCH (DESK RESEARCH)

This should be your first source of information. Generally, it will be the quickest way to gain an overall awareness of a situation. The quantity and quality of these data will vary, so the degree to which you can use desk research can vary. Typical areas to look for information in are:

1. PUBLISHED SOURCES
    - Trade bulletins (e.g. *Scrip*, *Clinica*, *Medistat*, *Pharmaceutical Times* and *Pharmaceutical Marketing*).
    - Medical Information Services (Medlar, Adis Review, etc.).
    - Technical Journals.
    All these can provide excellent information sources.

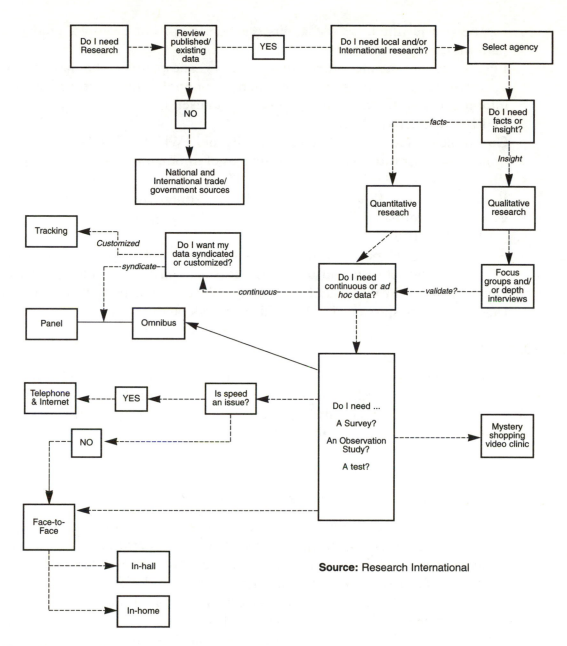

FIGURE 18 A MARKETING RESEARCH DECISION-MAKING PROCESS

2. COMPANY SOURCES

Apart from the normal sales and financial figures, you now have market reports available on-screen. These reports include selected information from IMS:

- Medical Data Index (prescription data);
- Pharmaceutical Index (unit sales data);
- Hospital Index (hospital sales data);
- Promotional Index (number of details/100 physicians).

Use of hard-copy audits supplement 'on-screen' data. There is much more information in hard copy *but* it is more difficult to access.

- Scripcount (prescription data);
- Media promotional spend at national level monitoring.

Also Medicare Audits (hospital data) and omnibus surveys. Furthermore, where it can be cost-justified, '*ad-hoc*' audits can be set up. For example, product referral patterns can be monitored!

Finally, do not ignore other areas, such as salespeople who have worked for competitors, medical staff, production personnel, and your colleagues. This information may be fragmentary, but is always useful.

3. PUBLIC ORGANIZATIONS

   Government statistics, although generally old, WHO, Chambers of Commerce, professional institutions are all good sources of information.

4. PRIVATE COMPANIES

   Best known are IMS and Kompass, although Mintel and other companies provide good audit information.

5. UNIVERSITIES

   The increasing link between companies and universities has opened up new sources of information. Sociologists and other specialists are constantly studying change in the environment, occupations and habits. An excellent and inexpensive way of obtaining a large survey is to sponsor a PhD candidate to work on the subject.

PRIMARY RESEARCH

This is also known as original or survey research. Where the data needed do not exist, or existing data are dated, inaccurate, incomplete or unreliable, the primary data will have to be collected. This involves greater cost and longer delay, but the data are usually more relevant to the issue at hand, and also accurate.

INTERVIEWS

Interviews can be *unstructured*, *semi-structured* or *structured*.

- *The unstructured interview* can be used either individually or with a group. It consists of introducing one or more general topics and allowing the participants to discuss them in their own words and from their own experience. It is extremely useful for gaining an initial 'feel' for a situation and obtaining the framework for more specific research. However, due to the random element, analysis is difficult. Information gained this way is always qualitative (i.e. cannot be statistically measured).

- *The semi-structured interview* is a stage further on. Discussions are now guided in a predetermined general direction. A guide is produced outlining key question areas and showing the direction to be taken. However, the interviewer has freedom to rephrase, reword, or rearrange them according to the needs of the moment. They are very useful when you need to examine a specific subject in depth. However, the information still tends to be qualitative, and analysis is difficult.

- *The structured interview* is the final quantifiable stage. The questions are preset and no deviation in the words or order is allowable. Its major use is in providing 'hard' data.

DATA COLLECTION CHANNELS

Tables 17(a), (b) and (c) show the key advantages and disadvantages of the face-to-face mailing, and telephone methods.

Table 17(a)   Advantages and Disadvantages of Data Collection Methods

---

FACE-TO-FACE

- Used when you need to qualify response
- Allows for detailed targeting of respondents
- Can be expensive – depends on ease of access to respondents
- Can be time-consuming
- Allows for a detailed study to be undertaken including open-ended questions
- Allows samples, show cards and other stimulus material to be used
- Can last up to 60 minutes (optimum 20–30)
- Interviewing carried out in street, hall, surgery, hospital or home
- In drawing up the questionnaire and the briefing for the research team – assume they have no intelligence

---

Table 17(b)   Advantages and Disadvantages of Postal Collection Methods

---

POSTAL

- Allows for possible large samples using own lists or list brokers
- No control over response rates or time (response rates are low)
- Self-completion format necessitates simple question design
- Can be cost-effective
- Best for simple, limited information needs
- Who fills in the questionnaire?
- Are responders typical?

Table 17(c)   Advantages and Disadvantages of Telephone Collection Methods

---

TELEPHONE

- Allows for reasonably fast turnround
- Computer techniques (CATI) allows instant access to results and flexibility in questioning
- Gives improved access to people who work during the day
- Greater wastage of initial contacts
- Those without telephones are excluded
- Sometimes people reluctant to co-operate; easier to say 'no'
- Optimum length about 20 minutes
- Can be used to gain fast reaction to specific events
- Difficult to hold attention and to establish rapport

GROUP DISCUSSIONS/FOCUS GROUPS

Group discussions/focus groups are best used when the primary concern is understanding, rather than measuring (i.e. 'what?', 'why?', 'how?', not 'how many?'). They complement quantitative research and can be done before or after. The techniques used in a group discussion are derived from the therapeutic and diagnostic tools of the psychiatrist and clinical psychologist.

Typically, they involve small samples of customers which are not necessarily representative of larger populations and employ a wider range of techniques to collect data than simply structured, question-and-answer techniques. The *interpretation* of the findings from a group discussion is an integral part of data collection.

Given the degree of latitude and the need for instant recognition of important items, it is obvious that the key to success lies with the interviewers. They must be knowledgeable and aware. Particular skills are those of creating and maintaining rapport, stimulating, probing, summarizing, and balancing – but, above all, avoiding directing the discussion.

Tape-recording these discussions is essential. The role of the interviewer is very onerous and note-taking is merely another burden. Additionally analysis afterwards will reveal items that were missed *en route*.

What is to be avoided is the lack of homogeneity in a group – *never* put a senior with a junior in the same group if you want to gather all views.

Use focus groups to:

- conduct concept testing/triage;
- test advertising/copy;
- evaluate market strategy;
- test packaging/design;
- improve WWW site design;
- hold brainstorming/idea generation session;
- improve product development process.

SURVEYS

A survey is typically used to collect and analyse the opinions, perceptions and/or experiences of randomly-selected individuals. Surveys can also be used to collect demographic information. Internet surveys are fast becoming the most convenient means of obtaining up-to-date market information.

Use surveys to:

- test products and concepts;
- collect customer attitudes and opinions;
- conduct customer satisfaction studies;
- do any kind of quantitative research;

- evaluate new marketing strategies;
- understand buying behaviour;
- track product usage;
- gather segmentation data.

The use of an external agency

Where research is to be commissioned from an agency, the vital first step is a clear brief. This cannot be overemphasised: even the best agency cannot guess what information is needed, if the problem is expressed in a vague way.

A good brief includes:

- an outline marketing background to the problem or potential opportunity, including references to any relevant existing research and marketing data, stating *why* the research is being undertaken;
- a statement of the objectives for the research itself (what do you intend to find out);
- a detailed specification of what the research criteria will be for making a decision (action standard);
- notes on required timing;
- notes on cost limitations.

Clearly, the product manager should be responsible and accountable for writing this brief. As a starting point, it is helpful if you outline your objectives and provide some background to the problem or potential opportunity, i.e. what you want to do with the information. Furthermore, you should always check that the brief conforms with the research objectives.

The brief is submitted either by the market research department or the product manager to the chosen research agencies. If the work is specialized, there may be little choice of available agencies. In many cases, particularly where the company has a good, ongoing relationship with an agency, it alone will be asked for a proposal. Generalized criteria for the selection of any agency are complex, and it is often best to use an agency with whom the market research department are already familiar.

The agency will then prepare a detailed *research proposal* setting out the way in which the problem will be tackled and the information which will be collected. Estimates of cost, timings, etc., must also then be included.

After discussion, amendment and approval of the research proposal, the agency will *carry out the research and prepare a research report* of the findings.

The market researchers' perspective of the pharmaceutical industry

The majority of market research agencies work across a wide range of industries. However, some will have much more experience in the pharmaceutical/healthcare industry. The paradox is that the industry generally does not want its market research agency to be working for competitor companies and products, but *does* want to see some evidence of expertise in the relevant field.

WHERE DO THEY PERCEIVE THAT RESEARCH UNDERTAKING BY THE PHARMACEUTICAL INDUSTRY DIFFERS?

The pharmaceutical industry differs slightly from the FMCG sector in that the majority of research involves talking to physicians, nurses, and other healthcare professionals, rather than to the end-user.

Another way in which it differs is that the positioning work for a product starts at a time when even the company is not totally sure of what the product will deliver, that is before the results of Phase III.

The fact that the communication is directed to the customer (physician), as opposed to the end-user (patient), means that the industry tends to communicate the features of a product rather than the benefits.

If the industry want to start tackling the communication of the benefits of a product, there is a need to look at the motivation behind purchase/up-take of the product. This is the focus in the consumer industry, but not an approach that is common in the pharmaceutical industry.

HOW SHOULD PRODUCT MANAGERS ENSURE THAT THEY GET THE BEST RESULTS FROM THEIR MARKET RESEARCH AGENCY?

The market research agency needs to be seen as an integral part of the pre-marketing process. This is a new trend in the industry and not yet common. Companies are keen to rationalize and optimize the way they use external agencies.

Market researchers believe that, if they were part of the 'business group' as opposed to a 'task force', this would ensure that:

- they were called in earlier in the project and their work could truly be integrated with marketing;
- they could act, and be remunerated, as consultants, i.e. provide a true 'intellectual input' to the marketing effort.

HOW DO MARKET RESEARCHERS DESCRIBE THE TYPE OF WORK THAT THEY UNDERTAKE WITHIN THE PHARMACEUTICAL INDUSTRY?

This falls largely into three categories, none of which is healthcare-specific. This is described as:

1. *strategic research*: this includes strategic concept research, and positioning statements;

2. *tactical research*: this involves undertaking research that helps you execute elements of the broader picture;

3. *ad-hoc projects*: these include research into packaging, representative details, etc.

WHERE IS THE RESEARCH MONEY SPENT IN THE PHARMACEUTICAL INDUSTRY?

The general opinion is that there is more money spent on execution of strategy than on developing the strategy which, in their words, 'seems back to front', whereas the belief is that it should be the other way round. Marketing research should always be strategic rather than tactical. The later you tackle an issue in the marketing process, the more likely you are to find out that you have to review some of your earlier decisions, because the findings of the research have highlighted aspects of the broader picture which you have not considered before.

Another area in which there is significant expenditure is in the pre-marketing phase for a product.

Also, a huge amount of money is spent on tracking/scripcount-type research to obtain basic information on drug performance, for example.

IS THERE A DIFFERENCE IN THE TECHNIQUES USED IN THE PHARMACEUTICAL INDUSTRY?

The techniques used are usually imported from FMCG, and slightly modified to suit the needs of the pharmaceutical industry.

When undertaking qualitative research in group meetings, you must bear in mind that the reaction you can get can be provoked by the group dynamic, and that, if you upset a doctor while carrying out the research, the consequences are far greater than if you upset one single beer drinker. A final point worthy of note is that, when analysing, emphasis can be put in words instead of the meaning. Typically, psychology techniques are used to analyse the meaning behind the word.

Examples of techniques used in quantitative research: conjoint analysis; sophisticated modelling; regression analysis.

WHAT ARE THE LIMITATIONS YOU ARE WORKING TO WHEN WORKING WITH A PHARMACEUTICAL CLIENT?

REAL

Patient research. This is an area where agencies have to be careful because of data protection rules and confidentiality issues. Another constraint lies in the fact that pharmaceutical people do not usually have experience outside the industry, and thus the market research has to face a degree of conservatism. Finally, it also appears that the industry believes in sales strategy more than brand strategy – which is probably why the research emphasis is on execution of strategy rather than on the strategy itself.

Physicians won't go to group meetings. Opinion leaders have to be dealt with in a 'meeting' framework, not with a workshop-type approach. Finally, the industry cannot be challenging or innovative because they might upset their customers.

IS THERE A GAP BETWEEN WHAT YOU CAN OFFER AND WHAT THE INDUSTRY USES YOU FOR?

Yes, we are typically used to go out and gather data. The consultancy role (or offering strategic marketing advice) is an area in which the pharmaceutical industry could use us more. Also, we are not often asked to communicate the research findings to the different audiences in the organization.

WHAT IN YOUR OPINION IS THE ROLE OF THE MARKET RESEARCH AGENCY *v* THE CLIENT?

The general view is that the market research agencies should be responsible for the planning of the research, the data-gathering and analysis, providing consultancy services and, therefore, somehow help in solving the marketing issue. Also, their role should be in communicating the findings to the different audiences in the organization.

The client's responsibility, on the other hand, is to communicate a clear brief as well as the entire agenda (internal issues and the objectives) and to put the right persons in front of the agency at the agency briefing meeting. Their words 'too often the marketeer is not present and we end up with the wrong brief'. Where an internal marketing research department exists, its role should be administrative, i.e. providing the client with an appropriate agency, and it may well take on the planning role, i.e. co-ordinating all the research and identifying areas where further research could be useful.

DO YOU FEEL THAT THERE IS GENERALLY A COMMON UNDERSTANDING OF EACH OTHER'S ROLE?

Yes, generally speaking. In practice, however, the agency sometimes finds itself in a complex situation if the agency – acting as a consultant – pinpoints an issue which then requires a review of the project objectives. This is why you need a good relationship with the client.

WHAT ELEMENTS DO YOU NEED TO HAVE IN PLACE TO OPTIMIZE YOUR CHANCES OF ACHIEVING SUCCESSFUL RESEARCH?

To optimize success the research agency needs to:

- have a good brief;
- share all the information;
- have a clear view of the 'deliverables' (e.g. client's expectations – they must be aware of the limitations of the methodology we use). Clients believe that once the interviews have been completed, most of the work has been done. In actual fact, the most difficult part of the research process is still to come;
- be clear on how/why they will use the information.

The client needs to:

- know the strengths and weaknesses of the agency they are working with;

- talk to the agency before they even produce the brief;
- build a strong relationship with the agency;
- build trust;
- try to avoid imposing time constraints.

HOW DO YOU EVALUATE THE SUCCESS OF A PROJECT?

There appears to be no formal process for evaluating the success of market research in place. Typically, the agency sees it as the client's responsibility to assess the success, and more important, to set the parameters at the briefing stage (e.g. audience, agenda, etc.).

Failure is perceived to be easier to assess, because failure means research is not actioned.

On a general basis market research agencies get anecdotal feedback.

10

Implementation and Control

Introduction

The first part of this chapter outlines the 'implementation and control' section of your marketing plan, which is aimed at providing top management with key information on your product plan proposal and at linking all activities which must take place, as proposed in the plan, in a format which will help you control them.

When top management at corporate, international or company level review marketing plans, they ask themselves the following questions:

- How much will we sell? Is that a realistic objective?
- How do these sales objectives relate to the market situation? How do these sales objectives relate to our competitive position?
- How much money will we need to spend to achieve these objectives?
- How much profit will we make?
- What key assumptions have been made to arrive at the forecasts and product objectives? Do we agree with these?
- What if *X* (e.g. a planned price increase or product launch) does not happen as planned? What impact will this have on sales and profits? What action/strategy shall we need to adopt then?

To answer these questions quickly, top management need only refer to the *executive summary* in your marketing plan, in which you will have included:

- the revenue objectives supported by the plan assumptions;
- a product P.&L.;
- a summary of the business situation;
- the proposed strategy;
- the CSF and your marketing objectives;
- a summary of the key actions that will be required.

In the second part of this chapter, we are concerned with making sure that all activities which you intend to happen in the following year *do in fact take place*. To that end, you are asked to prepare an action timetable and a performance feedback form which you can use throughout the year as an implementation-and-control document.

Product profit-and-loss statement (P.&L.)

This part of the marketing/product planning is concerned with the financial summaries of the individual steps and actions to be implemented in the planning year, and beyond that for the total number of years covered by the strategic marketing plan. Your product profit-and-loss statement provides the means by which you and your management colleagues can assess the revenues and profits that are projected for the product. Tables 18 and 19 show the generic form of a revenue template and the product P.&L.

As you are writing your plan and making forecasts, you are undoubtedly making certain assumptions: for example, we will get a price increase of 12 per cent in January; we will be granted registration for this new product by 1 July; raw material costs will be 4 per cent over current level; and so on. These must now be stated so that top management are aware of them, and to allow for the preparation of contingency plans and re-forecasts, if some of these assumptions prove not to be right or acceptable. Your key assumptions appear immediately below or adjacent to the P.&L. statement.

Summary of key objectives/actions

Table 20 enables you to summarize the CSFs, the objectives and key activities that must be undertaken to implement. A chart similar to this one must be included in your strategic marketing plan.

To carry out the marketing plan for your product, you should bring together in a timetable the various actions that need to be taken by you in the following year. This will help you list these key actions for the plan year. For each action listed you should note the related costs, so that you have in hand a spending control document for your yearly budget.

Against objective simply state how you will measure whether the CSF is managed effectively.

Performance feedback

Once the objectives have been set, the product strategies formulated, and the marketing and promotional plans set in motion, you must ensure that there is a control process which will enable you to monitor the performance of your product and to identify any parts of your plan where corrective action may be needed.

This means that you need to:

- set standards of performance against which actual results can be measured;
- fix times for the regular review of your plan;
- compare results against standards and identify variances;
- take corrective action to put the plan back on course or adapt the plan to meet changed circumstances.

TABLE 18 ANNUAL SALES FORECAST

PRODUCT:

Annual Sales Forecast

PRODUCT SALES DATA	Current Year −3	Current Year −2	Current Year −1	Current	Current Year +1	Current Year +2	Current Year +3
Volume (units)							
% growth							
Value							
Average unit price							
% growth							
Net sales							
% growth							
MARKET SHARE DATA							
% Volume Market Share							
% Value Market Share							
Market Position (e.g. No. 1, 2, etc.)							
Leading Competitors' Market Share %							

Key Assumptions:

TABLE 19 MARKETING PROFIT STATEMENT

Marketing Profit Statement

PRODUCT:

	Current Year −3	Current Year −2	Current Year −1	Current	Current Year +1	Current Year +2	Current Year +3
SALES							
Cost of goods							
Gross Profit							
Advertising (including A&M)							
Sales Promotion							
Market Research							
Total Marketing Expenses							
Professional Affairs							
Clinical Trials							
Outcomes Research							
Other							
Total Commercial Expenses							
Brand Contribution Level 1							
Sales Force Cost							
Consolidated Contribution							

Ratio Analysis:
Return on Investment
Return on Sales

TABLE 20   THE ACTION PLAN

PRODUCT:

ACTION PLAN																					
CSF:																					
Objective:																					
Activity	Key	Code	Budget Actual	Start	End	Resp	Jan	Feb	Mar	April	May	June	July	Aug	Sept	Oct	Nov	Dec	Impact

SETTING STANDARDS

The product plan contains specific, financial, marketing, sales, distribution and advertising objectives. These objectives provide the basis for the setting of standards in key areas. One of the important standards will be the annual targets: what your product will produce in sales, profits and market share. These are known as the *absolute standards*. They will tell you what has gone right or wrong but not *why*.

The second set of standards are the *moving standards*. These are the annual targets divided into whatever is a sensible division of the year (e.g. monthly/quarterly/half-yearly targets). Here again, although these more frequent indicators of performance will forewarn of deviations from your product targets, they will not show why performance is varying.

Thus, there is a need for a third set of standards – *diagnostic standards* – which tell you what is causing variations and why, so that you can take appropriate corrective action: for example, reviewing sales call levels, distribution channels activities, level of acceptance in the field of your promotional message, sales disparity by geographical region, and so on. The diagnostic standards will typically be set in relation to the *critical success factors*.

VARIANCE ANALYSIS

Variances are calculated by comparing actual results against preset standards. First, use cumulative totals so that individual monthly variations will tend to cancel each other out.

Second, moving annual totals (MATs) can be used by taking twelve months' performance up to and including the month in question. Because the same month of the previous year is deducted as each month is added, the trend in *moving annual total* will indicate present performance compared with the same period in the previous year.

Variance analysis can be done on what is called a 'Z chart', such as the one shown in Figure 19. This enables you to make comparisons on a single diagram of monthly performance against target, cumulative performance against target and, via the moving annual total, the present year versus the previous year.

The benefit of a good control system and feedback mechanism is that it enables the manager to identify quickly product performance variances and the true reasons for them, and to react to changed circumstances. By controlling your plan you will then be in a position to report monthly, and answer the following questions which may be raised by your top management:

- Are the plan objectives being met?
- What are the variances between budget and actual?
- What are the causes of these variances?
- What actions are being taken to correct them?
- Is a re-forecast/re-budget necessary?

These are the types of question which are usually asked monthly, but especially at other update review periods. A product manager is expected to know 'what is happening' with the product(s). The better your control system is, the more you will feel and appear to be in control of your product(s).

MONITORING AND CONTROL

Most forecasts are not 100 per cent correct, but it is important to keep the difference between actual and forecast as small as possible. It is essential, therefore, that constant monitoring takes place to improve forecasting ability.

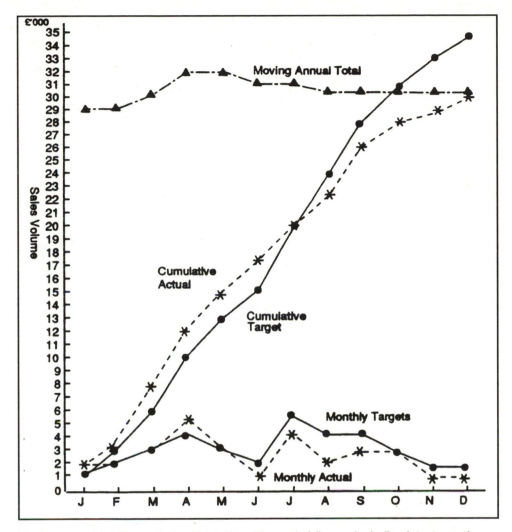

Moving annual totals are derived by taking 12 months' figures including latest month. Thus MAT for June covers period July last year to June this year. MAT for August is calculated by deducting August last year adding August this year. Therefore if total rises, performance is better than last year.

	ACTUAL SALES LAST YEAR	SALES TARGET THIS YEAR	ACTUAL SALES THIS YEAR	MOVING ANNUAL TOTAL (12 MONTHS TO DATE)
J	10,000	10,000	20,000	290,000
F	20,000	20,000	20,000	290,000
M	20,000	30,000	30,000	300,000
A	30,000	40,000	50,000	320,000
M	30,000	30,000	30,000	320,000
J	20,000	20,000	10,000	310,000
J	40,000	50,000	40,000	310,000
A	30,000	40,000	40,000	300,000
S	30,000	40,000	30,000	300,000
O	30,000	30,000	30,000	300,000
N	10,000	20,000	10,000	300,000
D	10,000	20,000	10,000	300,000
TOTAL	280,000	350,000	300,000	

Source: M.T. Wilson, *Managing a Sales Force*, 2nd edn, Aldershot, Gower Publishing, 1983.

FIGURE 19 THE Z-CHART

11

Writing the Plan

The importance of writing in business

In business, documents are a primary means of communication. Documents are written to:

- request action;
- inform (no action required);
- confirm agreement;
- summarize experience and information.

The benefits of good business writing are numerous:

- Well-written documents shorten the cycle of submission, consideration, decision and action. They get more action – faster!
- Attending to simplicity, clarity and brevity helps to sharpen the writer's thinking.
- Documents are an extension of the writer. A well-written document will tell the reader that you are a professional – the reader will respect your knowledge and judgment.
- Well-written documents are invaluable for providing the company with clear records. Managers can access factual information rather than rely on memories and opinions.

'Writing is an instrument for conveying ideas from one mind to another; the writer's job is to make the reader apprehend the meaning readily and precisely'

Sir Ernest Gowers – *The Complete Plain Words*

Prepare before you write

The importance of preparation in document writing is often undervalued. Thorough preparation can often improve the end result and reduce the number of draft documents written.

You may find the following guidelines useful:

- Know who your reader is and what they must do after reading the document. Effective communication of ideas depends upon recognizing that there is a difference between your reader's point of reference and your own – find out what they will need to know to understand the document.

- Define what key factors the reader will want to consider if they are to make a decision.
- Collect all relevant information relating to these factors. You cannot write an idea clearly until you have thought it out clearly. You cannot think it out clearly until you have all the information.
- Analyse the information and draw logical conclusions.
- Develop the document in outline form first. Outlining is the most important step in the writing process – it allows you to brainstorm ideas in a random order without worrying about logic, order, words and sentences. Once you have organized your ideas, you can concentrate on words and sentences. Outlining divides writing into two major elements – *what* you write, and *how* you write it.
- Divide the document into manageable chunks – do not try to write the first draft from start to finish in one sitting.

Basic formats

The format of a document will vary according to whether you are summarizing a research report, proposing a major launch of a product or writing a monthly report.

The benefits of using a standard format for each type of document are twofold:

- It enables the reader (e.g. marketing director) to make faster and more effective decisions across many brands. This is because they do not have to adapt to the particular style or format for each (e.g. marketing) manager.
- It enables the writer to organize their thoughts quickly. Time is not spent developing a new format.

Words, sentences, paragraphs, facts and tables

Use words which express the exact meaning you wish to convey. Use no more words than are necessary to do the job. Superfluous words waste your time, tire your reader and obscure the meaning of your document. Remember, words are only conveyors of information. Select words that are:

- short rather than long;
- familiar rather than unusual (e.g. jargon, foreign words);
- concrete rather than abstract;
- active rather than passive.

Keep sentences short and simple. By *short*, we mean number of words per sentence. Sentences should average 15–20 words. However, most sentences contain 25–35 words. Short sentences will help you to think clearly and the reader to take your meaning. By *simple*, we mean one major idea to a sentence. Two or more ideas per sentence confuses the reader (and sometimes the writer!).

Documents would be unreadable if they were not divided into paragraphs. The paragraph is essentially a unit of thought, not a certain number of sentences. The paragraph helps the reader by grouping sentences around a central idea.

Use facts and numbers instead of subjective judgment and opinion. Only use those facts and numbers which are relevant to the subject – you do not have to write down everything you know – only enough to convey the message.

Use tables in the document if:

- the numbers are complex and have interrelationships. The table will help the reader to understand the point being made;
- it will save the reader time;
- the reader will be using the tabulated information as a reference sheet.

Tables should be kept simple and should be fully explained. Do not expect the reader to deduce the meaning of a table.

A checklist for effective writing

IS THE DOCUMENT COMPLETE?

- Does it contain all the information necessary for the reader to make a decision?
- Is the information reliable and up-to-date?
- Does the document answer all questions raised?

IS THE DOCUMENT CLEAR AND PRECISE?

- An effective document only succeeds when the reader completely understands the message the writer is communicating.
- Have you used short and familiar words?

IS THE DOCUMENT CONCISE?

- The reader must understand your message as quickly and as easily as possible – you can make your point and be brief by eliminating unnecessary words and details.

IS THE INFORMATION ACCURATE?

- Is the information correct?
- Is the writing free from errors in grammar, spelling and punctuation?
- An imperfect document conveys a message to the reader, for example – several typos may raise questions about the thoroughness of thought or the time spent in checking the accuracy of the information.

IS THE PURPOSE OF THE DOCUMENT CLEAR?

- Does the reader know what they are supposed to do after reading the document?

A template for the marketing plan

Example Contents

SECTION 1	Executive Summary
SECTION 2	Situational Analysis/Key Issues
SECTION 3	Financial Objectives
SECTION 4	Strategy
SECTION 5	CSFs/Action Plan
SECTION 6	Measurement
SECTION 7	Contingency Plans

Glossary of Marketing Terms

Awareness

This refers to the situation of one 'having knowledge of' a product's existence. There are different levels of awareness. The level that is desirable is known as 'top of mind' awareness. That is, the product/service is one of the top three options that spring to mind immediately in the relevant situation.

Capability

Capabilities are the skills and disciplines which specifically apply to the business and have a direct and significant effect on competitiveness.

CD-ROMs

Their chief advantage is they contain much more information than a floppy diskette. CD-ROMs are relatively inexpensive to duplicate. The disadvantage is that not every computer has a CD-ROM drive and the speed of the CD-ROM drive varies from one computer to another.

Community Relations

This is becoming an increasingly important aspect of PR. Companies wanting to serve their communities successsfully have to demonstrate commitment and consideration for the needs of the community . . . whether it be local, national or global.

Competition

This includes any company which provides or will be in a position to offer a product/service or solution that meets the customer's needs.

Crisis Management

All companies face the possibility of becoming involved in a crisis situation which can damage their financial health and/or public image. A plan is needed to help you handle such possibilities.

Critical Success Factors (CSFs)

The critical success factors are the most important conditions that a business must identify and satisfy if it is to be an effective competitor and thrive. They are not objectives in themselves, but they are the factors that play a major role in guiding the company towards business success.

Differentiation

A situation where the company or brand is perceived as unique or better than its competitors. Differentiation may be product quality, distribution, or after-sales service. In marketing terms, this is known as differentiated marketing.

Dissatisfaction

Satisfaction is a function of the closeness between the prescriber's expectations and the product's perceived performance. Dissatisfaction is where the product falls short of expectations.

Electronic Mail

Also known as e-mail. Some e-mail systems allow you to send attachments which (sometimes) could include graphics and/or other elements. E-mail systems can be limited to organizations.

Fax-on-Demand

A fax-on-demand system enables people to call a telephone number, enter touch tone codes and have specific information sent to them via a fax machine.

Field

Therapeutic area(s) for which the product presents the relevant indications – indications which are adopted in practice.

FMCG

Fast-moving consumer goods, i.e. products such as tea, coffee, bread, butter, washing-up liquid, detergents.

Influence

Any person or market characteristic which has/could determine the nature and/or shape of the market potential.

Innovation

A unique or creative idea that attracts the customer/consumer's attention, gets a reaction and sets your product/service apart from the competition.

Issue

Opportunities for which the company is not competitive, and/or threats.

Issues Management	Sometimes a company or product can be adversely affected by an issue that is controlled by outside forces. Misinformation associated with this issue can cause negative publicity about the product and/or company. Thus it is important to take an active role in discovering what social, political and economic issues are important and relevant to your business and marketing communications interests. You need to manage proactively the issues that are important and the way the company/product is perceived within the business community.
Key People	Clinical or non-clinical people who it is believed will have a significant influence on prescribing either directly, or indirectly.
Mailing Lists	These are closely related to newsgroups. Instead of subscribing to a newsgroup, you can choose to subscribe to an electronic mailing list on the subject. When you do, you automatically receive all the postings for a particular subject in your e-mail box. Whoever establishes an electronic mailing list can establish its parameters and, if they so desire, control its content.
Marketing Skills	The set of skills required to plan and execute the conception, pricing, promotion, and distribution of ideas, goods and services to create exchanges that satisfy individuals in the organization.
Media relations and publicity	Helping a company become the news instead of simply reacting to it requires extensive knowledge of the news and trade media and having many key media contacts. Relationships with the media, typically, need to be supported by providing valuable information through press releases, feature stories, pitch letters, news conferences, media tours and media kits.
Media Relations Training	Saying the wrong thing at the wrong time to the wrong member of the media can have disastrous effects. To be an effective communicator, any employees who are required to speak to the press need training, and should be provided with the do's and don'ts of working with the media.

Multimedia Kiosks	This is an interactive device placed at a central location that allows users to access information and/or place an order. Multimedia kiosks offer easy access by people who pass by the location, they can hold a lot of information and can be programmed to do almost anything. The disadvantage is cost.
Multivariate Methods	In marketing there are six main sets by which a market can be analysed: factor analysis; latent analysis; cluster analysis; correspondence analysis; multidimensional scaling; and conjoint analysis.
Need	A requirement, or basic human motivation which a customer must meet or satisfy in order to achieve their goals.
Objective	A quantified expression of what it is we are trying to reach. Typically, they are Specific, Measurable, Ambitious, Realistic and Timed: SMART.
Opportunity	A feature of the environment that is attractive. Opportunities will include trends which could, potentially, have a positive effect on the market because they will increase or facilitate access to the market. 'Opportunity' is independent of the fact that the company can, or cannot, meet the needs identified.
Positioning	A statement about where the product should be used.
Potential	The amount of business that might be realized by the players in the market if the total population who could benefit from a therapeutic approach had access to the treatment.
Professional Relations Plan	The New Product Development Team's tactical plan which supports the implementation of the strategy.
Publicity Tracking and Evaluation	A solid system for tracking and evaluating any coverage is important. This helps you maintain relationships with the media as well as measuring the return on your public relations investment.
ROI	Return on Investment.

Scenario (planning)	A set of assumptions about trends and how they will impact on the future. The scenario might also include forecasts about events that are likely to take place in the future in relation to a specific company, an industry or an economic activity.
Sector	An area/part of the market.
Segment (market)	A constituent portion of the market where the people within it have identical/similar needs or requirements.
Special Events	The company and/or product's exposure can be maximized by making pre- and post-event media contacts, arranging press interviews at the event, setting up press events and designing press kits.
Strategy	The thrust or focus of the company for future business. The scope of products and market segments that will/will not be considered. How the products will be positioned within the market segments. The source of (sustainable) competitive advantage.
Strength	Elements within the company's control that are required to manage the opportunities or threats and where the company's position – with regard to these elements – has been interpreted to be stronger than relevant competitors.
Tactics	A set of activities that will need to be undertaken in order to support the implementation of a strategy.
Threat	A feature of the environment which is unattractive because it could have a damaging effect on the market. It could be either through reducing market potential, or through closing the windows of opportunity.
Trends	Identified or forecast patterns of change over time.
Unmet Need	Need(s) which are not satisfied by the existing players in the market.

Usenet

These are so called 'newsgroups' on the Internet. Think of the newsgroups as discussion groups. Newsgroups are divided into several broad categories. When you subscribe to a newsgroup, you can read messages posted by other subscribers, respond to or supplement a currently posted message.

Weaknesses

Elements within the company's control that are required to manage the opportunities or threats and where its position – with regard to these elements – has been interpreted to be weak or weaker than relevant competitors.

The World Wide Web

Commonly referred to as WWW or 'The Web'. This is the part of the Internet that combines text and graphics (and sometimes sound and video). Pages on the Web feature hypertext links (words and phrases) and graphics you can click on with your mouse to go to additional pages or information. This is the portion of the Internet generating the most excitement and commercialization. Although the Web receives a lot of attention, it is important to bear in mind that not everyone who uses the Internet accesses or has the ability to access the Web.

Index

absolute standards 129
account executives 103–4
action plans and timetables 5, 7, 75, 90, 129
added value for customers 38
advertising 93–4, 103–4
    ABPI Code of Practice 109
advertising agencies 103–9
agencies, external 100
    consultancy role 120, 122
    evaluation of 105–8, 111–12, 123
    for market research 119–20
    for public relations 108–9
    functions of 103–4
    relationships with 110
Alpin & Barrett 83
analgesics 40
Ansoff matrix 63–4
attractiveness of market segments 24–30, 49, 67
audit information 115–16
'available' markets 23–4
awareness of the product 137

bargaining power 27–9, 32
'benefit' segmentation 19
benefits of products see products
'best case' strategy 77
best fit, line of 84
Boots (company) 82
Boston Consulting Group (BCG) 65
branding 101–2, 109–10
briefing an agency 103–5, 111, 119, 122
budgeting 100

capability 137
    distinctive 41–6
'cash cows' 28
CD-ROMs 137
champions for products 91–2
change
    attitudes to 2
    coming from outside the company 30
Coca Cola 66
communications strategy 93–4, 100–101, 109–11
community relations 137
company audit 6–7, 37, 41–7
    example of 46
company objectives 62
COMPAQ (company) 16
competitive advantage 2, 6–7, 17, 37–8
    customers' perceptions of 21
    from branding 102

scoring scale for 51
sources of 41–2
competitive environment 12, 25–6, 32–3
competitive marketing 69
competitive strategy model 65
competitors 137
    direct and indirect 15
    evaluation of 22–3
    intense rivalry from 26
    potential 16
consumer groups 32
consumers see customers
control systems 126–30
consultancy role for agencies 120, 122
cost leadership 65
creative strategy and creative output 94, 99, 103–4,
        109–11
creative thinking 5, 91
crisis management 137
critical success factors (CSFs) 5, 7, 89, 138
    definition of 87
    number of 88
customer focus 15–16
customer segmentation 68–9
customers
    attitudes of 20–21, 32, 55
    bargaining power of 27–8, 32
    characteristics of 17–18
    expectations of 32, 39
    information required by 68
    loyalty of 19–20
    needs of 6, 15, 17, 21, 39
    partnership with 27
    perceptions of 38–40, 55
    readiness to buy 20

data collection methods (for marketing research)
        117–18
decision-making, proactive and reactive 3
demographic factors in the external environment
        31
demographic segmentation 18
departmental co-ordination 4, 5, 91
desk research 114–16
diagnostic standards 129
differentiated and undifferentiated marketing
        65–9, 138
differentiation of products 39, 50
disposal of companies 8
dissatisfaction with a product 138
distribution channels xvi, 102–3

diversification 8, 65
documentation 11, 133–6
'dogs' 28
Duphar (company) 83
dynamics of the marketplace 22, 28–9

Eco washing-up liquid 67
economic environment 12, 31
electronic mail (e-mail) 138–9
'emotional' selling propositions 97
employees
    attitudes and expectations of 31
    availability and quality of 31
environment, ecological 33
environmental analysis 6, 30–34, 74
    purpose of 31
Eprex 102
executive summaries 125
exponential smoothing 84–5
external environment 30–33

face-to-face data collection 116–17
fax-on-demand 138
FCMG (fast-moving consumer goods) 138
feedback on performance 125
financial objectives 7–8, 88–9
flat organizational structures xv
focus groups 114, 118
Ford Motors 66
full market coverage 66
functional organization 91
future developments 13

gap analysis 80
G.D. Searle (company) 8
General Foods 17
geographic segmentation 17–18
Girolami, Sir Paul 8
Glaxo Holdings 8, 82–3
government regulation 32
government statistics 116
graphs, use of 30
group discussions 114, 118
growth/share matrix 26, 28

'habit' of customers 29, 80
high-quality products 102–3
historical review of markets 12
'horizontal' operation 91

IMS 116
internal analysis 37–47
Internet, the 118, 142
interviews for market research 116
investment decisions 81–3, 87
issues management 139

Kompass 116

learning points 81
life cycles of products 69
Lloyds Pharmaceuticals 83
Losec (company) 67
loyalty of customers 19–20
Lucozade 99

Mac throat lozenges 69
market, definition of 12, 15–16
market analysis 6, 22–30
    information for 24, 29–30
market development 27, 65
market forecasts 73–5
market opportunities 23–5, 140
    definition of 24, 34
    examples of 51
    exploitation of 47
    scoring scale for 51
market orientation 15–16
market penetration strategy 64
market potential 15, 22–4, 71
market research agencies 119–23
market segmentation 6, 12, 15–16
    concentrating on a single segment 66
    definition of and criteria for 16–17
    extent of 21
    multiple targeting within 22
    myths and realities of 21–2
    reasons for 21–2, 94
    types of 17–21
market share, forecasting of 78–80
market specialization 66
marketing mix 93–4, 101
marketing objectives 7, 88–90
marketing plans
    benefits from 2
    content of 1–2, 125
    information required for 12
    model format for 12
    need for 3
    objectives of 4
    steps in creation of 5–7
    template for 136
marketing research 113–23
    decision-making process 115
    for the healthcare industry 120–22
    qualitative and quantitative 114
Marks and Spencer 18
Maxwell House coffee 17
media relations 139–40
media strategy 101
medical directors of pharmaceutical companies
    109
Medicare Audits 115
mergers xv
'message' 94
    content and structure of 97–8
    source and credibility of 98–9
    see also differentiation of products
Minoxidil 15
Mintel 116
mission statements 8–9
Monsanto Chemicals 8
'moral' selling propositions 96–7
'most likely' strategy 77
moving annual totals 130–31
moving averages 84
moving standards 129
multimedia kiosks 140
multivariate methods 140

natural monopolies 37–8
new entrants to the marketplace 26–7, 32

new markets, exploitation of 65
new or improved products 12, 31, 64
new technologies 31
newsgroups 139, 142
niche strategies 21

objectives 62–3, 140
    financial 7–8, 88–9
    marketing 7, 88–90
'occasion' segmentation 19
omnibus surveys 115
one-to-one selling 98
opportunities *see* market opportunities
organizational structure xv, 9, 91
originality of creative material 111
OTSW analysis *see* SWOT analysis
outlining of documents 134
ownership, sense of 91

5 P's of successful marketing 89
packaging xvi, 33, 99, 101–2
paragraphs 135
patient research 121
penetrated markets 24
Pepsi Cola 99
perceptual maps 40
performance/importance matrix 88
performance management 5–8
pharmaceutical companies
    financial results 82–3
    medical directors 109
pharmaceutical industry, constraints in 109–10
planning cycle, stages of 9–12
political environment 12, 32
Porter, Michael 26, 65
positioning of products 38–40, 50, 101–2, 140
    in healthcare industry 120
    parameters for 40–41
post, data collection by 117
potential market 15, 23–4
pricing xvii, 29, 102
primary research 116–19
prioritization of activities 49, 87
proactive and reactive decision-making 3
product audit 6, 37–41
product development 39
product forecasts 75–8
product managers xvi, 91, 110–111, 119
product objectives 63
product orientation 15–16
product specialization 66
product strategy 61–3, 67–9
product symbolism 101
products
    benefits of 15, 19, 101, 120
    customers' attitudes to 21, 38–40
    user statuses and usage rates 19
professional relations planning 140
Profit Impact of Marketing Strategies (PIMS) 102
profit-and-loss (P&L) statements 126
profitability 81–2
promotional activity 29, 39, 93–4
    options for 'mix' of 95–6
    strategy for 99–100
Prozac 16
psychographic segmentation 18–19

public relations (PR) agencies 108–9
publicity tracking and evaluation 140

'qualified' market 23–4
qualitative and quantitative research 114
quarterly review of forecasts 80–81
'question marks' 28

'rational' selling propositions 97
'readiness to buy' 20
Reckitt & Colman 82
regression analysis 84, 121
research *see* marketing research
resource allocation, scope for 3
results, forecast compared with actual 80
return on investment 81–3, 102, 141
    for pharmaceutical companies 83
review of forecasts 80–81
Revlon, Charles 15
ROI *see* return on investment

sales forecasting 71–85
    bottom-up or top-down 71
    functions of 72
    overview of methods 83–5
sales potential 71
sanity checking 78
scenario planning 34, 141
segmentation *see* market segmentation
selective specialization 66
sentences, length of 134–5
simplicity in communications 111
situational analysis 4, 7, 12, 50
SMART criteria 63, 140
SmithKline Beecham 82–3
social environment 12, 31–2
special events 141
specialization strategies 66
standard formats for documents 134
standard-setting 129–30
'stars' 28
strategic assets 41
strategic behaviour 30
strategic intent 68
strategic options 7
    generation of 63–7
    inputs to 22, 30, 34, 38, 41, 47
Strategic Planning Institute 102
strategic research 120
strategy 4, 50, 87–92, 101, 141; *see also*
    communications strategy
strengths
    examples of 52
    identification of 47
Strepsils 69
subsidiary companies 10
substitute products 27, 32
suppliers, bargaining power of 28–9, 32
surveys for market research 118–19
SWOT analysis 49–59
    application of 88–9
    function of 50
    marketing decisions based on 59
    ranking of key factors 53–5
    strategic decision grid 55
    tabulation of 53

tables, use of 30, 135
tactical plans 90
tactical research 121
tactics 50, 63, 141
tape-recording of discussions 118
target audience 15, 24, 50, 68
targets 129–30
team dynamics 107
technological environment 31
telephone, data collection by 117
threats 141
    definition of 24, 34
    expectations about 54
    making markets unattractive 27–9
    management of 37, 41
Tie Rack 67
time series analysis 84
timetables 125–6, 129
TNT (company) 16
trend forecasts 73–5, 84
turnover of pharmaceutical companies 82

underlying trend *see* trend forecasts

uniformity in planning systems 11
unique selling proposition (USP) 97, 110, 112
universities, links with 116
usage rate of a product 19
usenets 143
user status for a product 19

variance analysis 130
vertically-organized companies 91
Vestric (company) 8
visualization of the message 98

weaknesses 47, 142
Wellcome Foundation 8–9, 82
Westminster Laboratories 83
World Wide Web 142
written documentation 12, 133–6

Z charts 130
Zantac 16
'zero-based' strategy 77